JUDGE FOR YOURSELF
MARTIN
LUTHER KING

CHRISTINE HATT

Evans

Published in this edition in 2009
by Evans Brothers Limited
2A Portman Mansions
Chiltern Street
London W1U 6NR

Printed in China by WKT

British Cataloguing in Publication Data
Hatt, Christine
    Martin Luther King. – (Judge for yourself)
    1.King, Martin Luther, 1929–1968 2.Afro-American civil
    rights workers – Biography – Juvenile literature 3. Civil
    rights workers – United States – Biography – Juvenile
    literature
    I.Title
    323.1'196'073'092

ISBN 978 0 237 53624 4

CREDITS

Consultant: Dr John A. Kirk, Royal Holloway College,
University of London
Editor: Jinny Johnson
Design: Mark Holt
Maps: Tim Smith
Production: Jenny Mulvanny
Picture research: Julia Bird

PICTURE CREDITS

For permission to reproduce copyright pictorial material,
the author and publishers gratefully acknowledge the
following:

t–top, *c*–centre, *b*–bottom, *r*–right, *l*–left

Corbis: 4, 12, 15, 19, 20, 22, 23, 26*b*, 27, 33, 34*r*, 35*b*, 37,
41*b*, 42, 43, 46, 49, 53*b*, 57

Hulton Getty: 5, 6*t*, 7, 10, 11*b*, 13, 14, 16, 17*b*, 18, 24, 25,
28, 34*l*, 35*t*, 36, 39, 44, 47, 53*t*, 54, 55, 56

J. S. Library International: 8

Mary Evans Picture Library: 9, 11*t*, 17*t*

Topham Picturepoint: 21, 26*t*, 29, 31, 32, 38, 41*t*, 45, 48,
52, 58, 59, 60, 61

ACKNOWLEDGEMENTS

For permission to use copyright material for the
documents, the author and publisher gratefully
acknowledge the following:

p.42, 44, 49: From *The political Philosophy of Martin
Luther Ling, Jr,* by Hance Walton, as published by
Greenwood Publishing Group Inc. in 1971. Reproduced by
permission of Greenwood Publishing Group inc.

p.47, 52, 54: From *The Words of Martin Luther King, Jr.,* as
published by Harper Collins in 1984. Reprinted by
arrangement with the estate of Martin Luther King Jr, c/o
Writers House as agent for the proprietor. Copyright
1963 Martin Luther King Jr., copyright renewed 1993
Coretta Scott King.

p.48: From *Causes and Consequences of the African-
American Civil Rights Movement,* by Michael Weber,
published by Evans Brothers Limited in 1997. By
permission of Evans Brothers Limited.

p.49, 50, 52, 53 and 61: From *A People's History of the
United States* by Howard Zinn published by Longman in
1980. By permission of Pearson Education Limited.

While every effort has been made to secure permission to
use copyright material, Evans Brothers apologise for any
errors or omissions in the above list and would be grateful
for notification of any corrections to be included in
subsequent editions.

VISIT OUR WEBSITE
Evans
www.evansbooks.co.uk

CONTENTS

JUDGE FOR YOURSELF

INTRODUCTION

The Baptist preacher and political activist Dr Martin Luther King, Jr. lived for fewer than 40 years, but in that short time he transformed the lives of black Americans. As a result of the non-violent campaigns he and others led in the USA during the 1950s and 1960s, black people gained not only new civil rights, but also a new sense of self-esteem following the bitter era of slavery and segregation (see pages 10 and 16).

This book looks at Martin Luther King and his activities in two different ways. In the first part, you can read the straightforward story of his life, from his birth as a preacher's son in Atlanta, Georgia in 1929 to his tragic assassination in Memphis, Tennessee in 1968. This part is divided into chapters in the normal way, and also includes feature spreads that highlight two special subjects, slavery in the USA until its abolition in 1865, and the following Jim Crow era in the South.

In the second part of the book, you can examine the main themes of King's life – for example, his belief in non-violent protest based on 'soul force', his struggle for black civil rights, and his opposition to the Vietnam War – much more closely. To help you assess King's ideals and actions for yourself, this part is divided into sections, each headed with an important question to consider. The first two pages below each question provide one possible answer, together with quotations, statistics and other facts to back it up. The next two pages provide a second potential answer, also with supporting evidence and information.

The question pages can be used in several ways. You may simply want to read them

King (centre, next to his wife Coretta) leads a major civil rights march through Selma, Alabama in March 1965 (see page 35).

CHANGING NAMES

During Martin Luther King's lifetime, black Americans were generally known as either Negroes or coloured people. During the mid-1960s, as the Black Power movement rose to prominence (see page 37), the term Afro-American became more popular, especially among black people themselves. Today, African American is widely used by members of all communities. To avoid any possible confusion, this book generally refers to black people as such throughout.

data to back up a particular view of the 1960s' civil rights legislation, of King's later attempts to help all the USA's poor, whatever their race, colour or creed, or of black people's struggle for equality since his death.

The question pages have another purpose, too. They are designed to show you that facts and statistics can be used to support completely different points of view. That is why historians have to sift through a great deal of material, from a wide variety of sources, before they can reach reliable conclusions about the past. Even then, answers are rarely clear-cut and may be overturned by new evidence. So, as you consider the questions, remember that neither of the answers provided may be completely correct. Using all the information in both parts of the book, and any more that you can find, it is up to you to judge for yourself.

through, look at both possible answers and sets of sources for each question, then make up your own mind. Perhaps you could also write down the reasons for your decision. Alternatively, the material could be used for a classroom debate between two groups, each arguing for a different answer. The pages may also serve as a prompt to further research. For example, you may wish to find additional

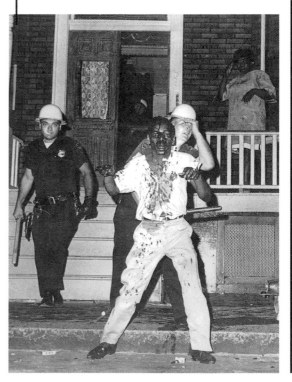

In northern US cities, ghetto conditions often led to unrest. This man was wounded during a riot in Newark, New Jersey in 1967.

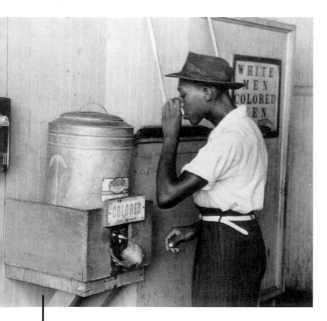

During the segregation era in the American South, blacks and whites had to use separate public facilities, including water coolers.

CHAPTER ONE

EARLY LIFE

Martin Luther King, Jr. was born on 15 January 1929 in Atlanta, Georgia, a state in the USA's Deep South. At first he was called Michael, after his father. But in 1934, Michael Sr. changed both his own and his son's name to Martin Luther, after the 16th-century German leader of the Protestant Reformation (see picture). As a child, however, the boy was usually known affectionately as ML.

German priest Martin Luther (1483–1546) was a founder of Protestant Christianity.

Asseruit Christum divina Voce LVTHERVS,
Cultibus oppressam restituitque fidem.
Illius absentis vultum hec depingit Imago,
Presentem melius cernere nemo potest.
— MARTINVS LVTHERVS. 1540.

FAMILY RELATIONSHIPS

ML grew up in a secure and loving black family, but there were some tensions. His fierce, strong-willed father dominated the household. The child of poor sharecroppers, Martin Sr. had struggled to gain an education and become pastor of Atlanta's Ebenezer Baptist Church. He intended to ensure that ML, his older sister Christine and younger brother Alfred Daniel ('AD') had a smoother path through life. But he demanded good behaviour and hard work in return. Like many parents of the time, he beat his children if he felt they had done wrong.

Two women also shaped ML's early years. The first was his mother, Alberta, whose father had been the previous pastor of Ebenezer Church. She was a quiet, gentle character who lived in her husband's shadow. The second was his maternal grandmother, a warmer, much more exuberant woman to whom he felt a special closeness.

ML's belief in God was nurtured not only by his father and other close relatives, but also by the wider 'family' he encountered in church every Sunday. There, some 4,000 members of Atlanta's black community found refuge from the mistreatment that was their daily experience in a state where segregation laws (see pages 16–17) were strictly enforced. During the sermons by Martin Sr., the congregation cried aloud in response, releasing all their pent-up sorrow and anger.

STARTING SCHOOL

During his pre-school years, then, ML moved between two

places of security – his comfortable home, which stood in the black middle-class ghetto of Sweet Auburn, and his father's church. Although the Great Depression hit the USA in the 1930s, plunging millions into poverty, Martin Sr.'s financial prudence and job as a pastor ensured that the King family never went short. But when ML began school in 1935, the harsh realities of life as a black person in the USA began to hit home.

The first shock came on the very day that he started at Younge Street Elementary School. His best friend, a white boy, was beginning his education at the same time. However, ML found that his playmate was not attending the same school, and that no other white children were either. Wanting to find out why, he called at his friend's house on the way home. But the boy's parents

Now a grown man and minister himself, Martin Luther King Jr. (far left) listens to his father preach at Ebenezer Baptist Church in 1964, just as he did when a boy.

informed him that the two were no longer allowed to play together because their son was white and he was 'coloured'.

ML rushed back to his own house to discuss this troubling development. His parents now realized it was impossible to shield him from the truth any more. So that evening, they explained the history of black people in the USA. As ML heard about the horrors of slavery (see page 10), the dashed hopes that followed abolition in 1865, and the Jim Crow laws that still operated in the South (see page 16), his childhood world fell apart. But his parents urged him to be strong and proud of his ancestry, saying: 'You must always feel that you are *somebody*.'

GROWING UP

After leaving Younge Street, ML continued his formal education at David T. Howard Colored Elementary School. Bright, hard working and popular, he was nevertheless regularly teased and called a 'shrimp' because he was so short for his age.

The film Gone with the Wind premiered in Atlanta in 1939, when King was ten. It portrays a romantic view of 19th-century life in the Deep South from the white viewpoint.

The success and acceptance ML found at school, church and home were not matched by his experience in the wider world. Almost every day, he noticed another way in which he and other black people were treated as second class. They had to sit in the back of buses, away from white passengers. They were refused service at the best restaurants and given the worst seats in cinemas. They were even obliged to use separate public toilets. In addition, white people spoke to them in an offensive manner, calling them 'niggers' and addressing grown men as 'boy'.

In December 1941, Japan attacked the American naval base in Pearl Harbor, Hawaii, and in response President Franklin D. Roosevelt led the USA into the Second World War. In 1942, against this uncertain background, ML began his secondary studies at Booker T. Washington High School. Now 13, he was starting to exhibit the usual anxieties and rebelliousness of adolescence. But in him they had a particular intensity. The injustice of racism preyed deeply on his mind, provoking a bitter anger. And his relationship with his domineering father was growing difficult.

MOREHOUSE COLLEGE

When he was just 15, a year earlier than was normal, ML won a place at Atlanta's prestigious, all-black Morehouse College. At first, he struggled academically at the college. This was partly because of his age. However, it also became clear that the education he had received at his previous schools was poor – despite his obvious abilities, he had the reading age of an 11-year-old. Rage at a system that considered black children too unimportant to educate properly drove ML's determination to catch up. Soon he was getting top marks in a wide range of subjects, including English and history. ML was developing in another way as well – he had discovered women and was soon stepping out with a string of girlfriends.

FINDING A VOCATION

Unlike many other Morehouse students, ML lived at home, and during this period, his complex relationship with his father came under even greater strain. ML loved Martin Sr. greatly. However, he was also resentful of his father's stubborn belief that he was always right. There were many clashes over minor issues – Martin Jr. loved dancing, for example, but his father thought it sinful. The growing religious differences between them, however, were much harder to resolve.

Martin Sr. was a fundamentalist – that is, he believed in the complete and literal truth of the Bible. But the more Martin Jr. studied and reflected, the more convinced he became that this simply could not be so. Thoughts of following in his father's footsteps as a preacher were now replaced by plans to become a lawyer who would fight against injustice through the courts. But then two instructors at Morehouse showed Martin – he had dispensed with the ML – that there was another way.

These two men were the college principal, Dr Benjamin E. Mays, and the head of religion, Professor George D. Kelsey. They helped the young scholar peel away the ancient mythology that overlay the Bible stories and so reveal the deep truths they contained. Mays and Kelsey also showed him how relevant those stories of struggle and salvation were to black people in the USA. Now Martin saw that he could be an honest minister of the Gospel while working to bring his people justice in the here and now. There was no need to copy his father's style of preaching or to accept his theology. He, Martin Jr., could serve God in his own way.

ORDINATION AND AFTER

Martin Sr. was delighted by his son's decision, but wanted to test Martin Jr.'s calling to make sure it was real. So in 1947, he arranged for the 18-year-old to preach a trial sermon at Ebenezer Baptist Church. The overflowing congregation was not disappointed. The teenager's arguments were rather lofty, and his preaching far more sober than his father's. But there was no mistaking his conviction and power.

Martin Jr.'s performance was good enough to satisfy his harshest critic. So it was with great pride that Martin Sr. ordained his son as a Baptist preacher on 25 February the following year and also made him assistant pastor at Ebenezer Baptist Church. Shortly afterwards, in the spring, Martin Jr. graduated from Morehouse and began to plan his future in more detail. But all he knew for sure was that he intended to engage in the struggle for racial justice, not quietly from the sidelines but in 'the very heat of it'.

Civil Disobedience, a book by American writer Henry Thoreau (1817–1862), introduced King to the idea of non-violent resistance.

This map of the USA shows all the important places mentioned in this chapter as well as others in later parts of the book.

SLAVERY

A Dutch sea captain brought the first black people to North America in 1619, and sold the 20 men to white Virginia settlers. But it was not until the 1680s, when serious labour shortages developed, that the transport of black people across the Atlantic from Africa greatly increased. At first, many blacks were treated no worse than poor white servants. But as the black population grew, so did racism. By 1700, the white community had enslaved most blacks and denied them even basic rights.

THE SLAVE TRADE

The demand for labour steadily grew in 18th-century North America, especially in the cotton and rice plantations of the South, and the slave trade flourished. Europeans took growing numbers of blacks prisoner in Africa, then chained them below decks in cramped, filthy ships, where disease spread rapidly. Many did not survive the transatlantic journey. By the time slaving trips had ended, about 600,000 Africans had arrived on the continent. Among them were the great-grandparents of Martin Luther King.

A scene in a slave ship travelling from Africa to the Americas.

BIRTH OF THE USA

In the late 18th century, the 13 British colonies of North America rebelled against the government in London and war broke out. The 1776 Declaration of Independence that announced the colonies' wish to be free of British rule boldly proclaimed: 'We hold these truths to be self-evident: That all men are created equal…' However, efforts by campaigners to apply this noble principle to blacks as well as whites by abolishing the slave trade came to nothing. In fact, as a result of Southern planters'

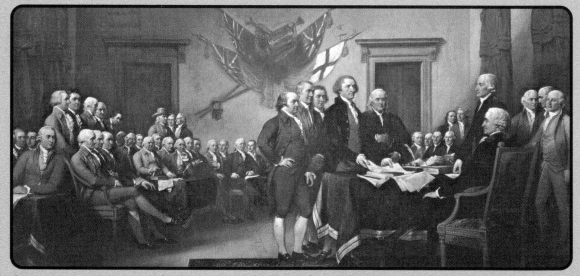

American statesmen sign the Declaration of Independence in 1776.

insistence, the 1787 constitution stipulated that the trade could not be banned before 1808.

NORTH V. SOUTH

The abolition of slavery itself was another matter. In the North, moral arguments supported by hard economics – the region was industrializing rapidly, so fewer farm labourers were needed – led to the outlawing of the institution in state after state. But in the South, the cotton industry was expanding (particularly after the invention in 1793 of the cotton gin, see below), fuelling demand for workers. After the slave trade's abolition in 1808, planters largely met this need by purchasing slaves from the North.

The cotton gin machine for separating cotton seeds from the fibres used for cloth.

ABRAHAM LINCOLN AND THE CIVIL WAR

In the mid-19th century, the differences between North and South became greater. Now the USA was expanding west and there were long debates in Congress about whether new territories should permit or ban slavery. In 1854, the Republican Party was founded in the North to oppose the institution's spread. Six years later, Republican Abraham Lincoln was elected president. This development prompted 7 (later 11) states in the South to leave the USA. Then, on 12 April 1861, forces of the southern Confederacy launched a war against the Union forces of the North.

THE EMANCIPATION PROCLAMATION

At the outset, Lincoln's war aim was to bring Confederate states back into the Union. But the conflict lasted far longer than he had expected. So in 1862, he decided to threaten the South's economic survival by proclaiming that if the Confederacy had not surrendered within 100 days, he would free all slaves in its territories. As there was no response, he issued the Emancipation Proclamation on 1 January 1863. It stated these slaves were '...then, thenceforward, and forever free', making the abolition of slavery in Confederate areas a second war aim.

ABOLITION AND AFTER

In January 1865, as the civil war was drawing to a close, President Lincoln steered an even more important anti-slavery measure through Congress. The historic Thirteenth Amendment to the constitution abolished slavery throughout the United States. On 9 April the same year, the civil war ended with the surrender of the Confederate forces. Now it seemed that black Americans in both the North and South could reasonably hope for a better future. But in fact their struggle had scarcely begun.

President Abraham Lincoln

SLAVE LIFE

Most black slaves in the USA laboured in the fields, either in the rice and cotton plantations of the South or on tobacco and arable farms farther north. Their working week usually lasted for six long days, sunrise to sunset, so they had little time for rest before the harsh round began again. Slaves in domestic service, many of them women, did not face the same physical demands. But they often had to deal with peevish, spiteful mistresses, and to fend off sexual approaches from masters. In addition, they were expected to work seven days a week.

Even when not working, slaves were treated with casual cruelty. Legally, they were simply a type of property that their masters could buy and sell at will. Slave-owners did not hesitate to split up families if it suited them, for example handing a mother over to one planter and her children to another. Punishments, from a simple reprimand to a severe whipping, were meted out for even minor misdemeanours. Masters generally provided their slaves with adequate food and housing, but little or no education. The vast majority of slaves were illiterate.

In the face of such constant trials, slaves struggled to preserve their dignity and self-esteem. They achieved this in particular by building strong, extended families, and by establishing networks of Christian churches. There they could worship in their own way and draw comfort from Bible texts that spoke of every individual's worth in the eyes of God and of the glories that awaited in heaven. It was this powerful religious tradition that Martin Luther King inherited.

CHAPTER TWO

COLLEGE YEARS

Once Martin Jr.'s Morehouse years were over, his father hoped he would settle down. What better future could there be than to marry his regular girlfriend, start a family, and eventually become chief pastor at Ebenezer Baptist? But Martin wanted instead to join Crozer Seminary, a theological college in the northern state of Pennsylvania. As he was now a mature 19-year-old, his father decided not to stand in his way.

STARTING COLLEGE

Martin Jr. arrived in Chester, the town where Crozer was situated, in the autumn of 1948. Full of intellectual curiosity, he was determined not to waste this opportunity to learn. As one of just six young blacks in a college of almost 100 students, he was also eager to prove himself.

From the beginning, King studied hard, arriving at classes punctually and spending long hours at his desk. But he was wary of showing his more fun-loving side – he had no wish to confirm the white stereotype of black men as jokers who never knuckled down to serious work. Then, just as he was starting to relax, an event occurred that highlighted the hatred some white students felt for Crozer's small black minority.

Among King's fellow students was a young white man from the southern state of North Carolina who believed that black people should not have the right to attend the college. One day, while he was still a freshman, the student returned to his room to find all his belongings in disarray. This was not an unusual event – at Crozer there was a tradition of 'raiding', that is completely ransacking, the rooms of new arrivals.

Despite a total lack of evidence, the North Carolinian decided this prank was a malicious attack, and that King was to blame.

The grand buildings of Crozer Seminary in Chester, Pennsylvania, where Martin Luther King studied theology from 1948 to 1951.

So he crashed into his fellow student's room shouting racist abuse and threatening to kill him with the gun he was carrying. King responded with magnificent calm, simply denying responsibility for the raid. Luckily, three other students then arrived and persuaded the intruder to drop his weapon.

The incident was soon reported to Crozer's student council, in the expectation that the offending young man would be dismissed from the college. But King refused to press charges, saying he was content with the apology his attacker had offered him. His restraint won him many friends – including the man who had threatened to shoot him dead.

SEMINARY STUDIES

As the months passed, King filled his head with new learning, from academic Christian theology to the ideas of secular philosophers both ancient and modern. Of special interest were the writings of Walter Rauschenbusch, a white Baptist preacher who had worked in the slums of late 19th-century New York. His book *Christianity and the Social Crisis* argued that Christians had a duty to tackle the poor's economic and social problems. It was not right to offer hope only for the after-life. The Kingdom of God that Jesus preached had to be established on Earth.

Shortly afterwards, King also became enthralled by the work of Mahatma Gandhi. Earlier in the 20th century, this Indian leader had mobilized the poverty-stricken masses of his country to fight against British colonial rule. They had done so successfully – India won its independence in 1947 – mainly by using the demonstrations, boycotts and other techniques of non-violent resistance that Gandhi had prescribed.

For King, this was an 'electrifying' revelation. He wanted to help American blacks win their freedom, not from foreign rule but from injustice. As a Christian, he had grave doubts about using violence for this purpose, but the pacifist alternative seemed a feeble means of confronting such a profound problem. Gandhi's tactics offered a third possibility. Collectively they were known in Hindi as *satyagraha*, that is 'truth force'. King later became convinced that this active force, not simply the passive absence of violence, was the way to defeat the world's evil.

Preaching practice

Despite the fact that it was integrated, Crozer was an essentially white environment. But in all his time there, King never forgot his roots in the black church. They were strengthened immeasurably by regular visits to nearby 'Barbour University'. This was not an academic institution, but the home of J. Pius Barbour, a distinguished pastor and friend of King's father, who had also been Crozer's first black graduate.

It was at Barbour's house that King refined his natural preaching abilities and learned to combine the raw power, emotion and faith of traditional black sermons with the more intellectual Crozer approach. By observing Barbour at work, he also discovered how to incorporate ideas about economics and politics into more obviously 'religious' addresses, and to discuss the complex notions of great thinkers without losing the attention of his audience. By the end of this training, his oratory was already able to captivate black and white listeners alike.

From Crozer to Boston

King's time at Crozer ended in June 1951, when he graduated first in his class with a BA in Divinity. The seminary prize for this achievement was a $1,300 scholarship to attend any place of postgraduate study that he chose. King's father indicated his approval by giving his son a green Chevrolet car. After spending the summer in Atlanta, the 22-year-

INTEGRATING THE ARMED FORCES

During the Second World War, about one million black Americans had served in the armed forces. However, they had not done so on the same terms as whites. In the army, black units were fully segregated and usually under the command of white officers. The navy was integrated, but blacks did not have the right to hold leadership roles. Black airmen served only in a specially established corps that trained at Tuskegee Airfield, Alabama (below).

In April 1945, as the war was drawing to a close, Democrat Harry S. Truman became US President. Over the next seven years, he made great efforts to force the issue of black civil rights onto the national agenda. His proposed anti-discrimination laws failed to survive Congress, thanks to the bitter opposition of members from the South. But Truman was able to make one significant change without congressional approval. In 1948, the President issued Executive Order 9981. It started the process of desegregating the US armed forces, and by the mid-1950s, the army, airforce and navy were all integrated services.

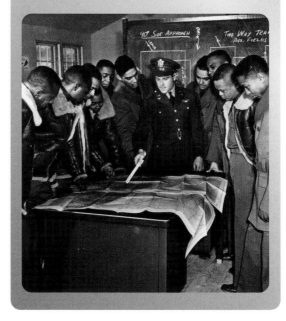

old headed north in this eye-catching vehicle to start at Boston University.

Once in Boston, King began to study Christianity in even greater depth than before, and to learn about a wide range of other subjects, from Islam to psychology. As usual, he thought deeply about each new topic, trying to see whether it had any relevance to his own life and beliefs. By spring 1953, he had completed all of his coursework, but decided to remain at the same university to prepare a Ph.D thesis.

LOVE AND MARRIAGE

It was by no means all work and no play in Boston. King often spent time at the Totem Pole jazz club. He also dined at restaurants where generous platefuls of fried chicken and other southern 'soul food' were served. But there was for many months no serious girlfriend in his life.

Finally, early in 1952, King decided that the time had come to find a lifelong partner. So he asked a friend, Mary Powell, if she knew of anyone suitable. Mrs Powell suggested Coretta Scott, a young woman from Marion, Alabama who was studying to be a singer at the New England Conservatory of Music. The same evening, King telephoned Coretta and arranged to meet her for lunch the next day.

King liked Coretta at once. She was pretty and bright, with a quiet inner strength. Coretta did not feel the same immediate attraction to King. He was short and very intense, questioning her about politics and other serious issues that most men would not even have mentioned on a first date. In any case, she was not a regular church-goer and thought preachers dull. But he slowly won her over. At the end of the date, King shocked Coretta by telling her that she would make an ideal wife.

From then on, King saw Coretta regularly, but she was reluctant to marry. She simply could not imagine herself as the demure, ever-smiling wife of a preacher and also

Martin and and his wife Coretta during their early years together. They were married in 1953.

knew that taking on this role would mean giving up her dreams of a career. There would not be time to help her husband with church business, raise a family and be a professional singer. In the end, King got his way. The couple wed on 18 June 1953 in the garden of Coretta's parents' house in Marion. After a brief honeymoon, both returned to Boston to complete their studies.

JIM CROW

'**Jim Crow**' was a black character in a song-and-dance act performed by American entertainer Thomas Rice. From the late 19th century, the term was also used to describe the system of segregation and related laws that grew up in the South after the American Civil War (see pages 10–11). Martin Luther King, Jr. dedicated his life to fighting Jim Crow.

INTRODUCING JIM CROW

After Reconstruction ended (see box), southern states slowly but surely reduced the civil rights of black people. First, they introduced measures to prevent blacks from voting. These included poll taxes, literacy tests (see page 24) and grandfather clauses. Next, they began to pass laws enforcing the segregation of public buildings and transport.

Black people also suffered from persecution by the Ku Klux Klan, a white supremacist organization founded in 1866. The first aim of the organization was to stop black people voting

In 1892, black carpenter Homer A. Plessy decided to challenge one of the segregation laws in Louisiana. So he sat in a whites-

Members of the Ku Klux Klan, a white supremacist organization.

only train carriage and let himself be arrested. The Supreme Court made the historic *Plessy* v. *Ferguson* ruling on the case in 1896. It stated Louisiana segregation laws did not violate the Fourteenth Amendment (see box and panel), as facilities for blacks were 'separate but equal'. After the ruling, more segregation laws were passed and the Jim Crow era began in earnest. In fact, black facilities were rarely equal, but the courts did not intervene.

FIGHTING BACK

Black people soon began to fight back. Among the first campaigners for better treatment was ex-slave Booker T. Washington. He became the first principal of the Tuskegee Institute in Alabama, an industrial

RECONSTRUCTION

Reconstruction began in 1865, after the Civil War. During this period, the southern states recovered from the fighting and rejoined the Union. At the same time, their governments tried to limit the rights of ex-slaves, while the federal government tried to increase them. In 1866, Congress passed a Civil Rights Act that gave blacks 'full and equal benefit' of all laws relating to themselves and their property. After imposing military rule in the South in 1867, it also managed to introduce the Fourteenth and Fifteenth Amendments to the Constitution (see panels). State governments with black members were elected, too, and strengthened black rights.

In the 1870s, intimidation of black voters and a white backlash allowed Democratic Party members who opposed racial equality to regain control of most southern governments. The situation became worse for blacks after the 1876 presidential election. The result was disputed, and southern white Democrats would accept the victory of Republican candidate Rutherford B. Hayes only if they were given the right to rule in the South without further federal interference. In 1877, the last federal troops left the region and Reconstruction ended.

THE FOURTEENTH AMENDMENT
(Adopted 1868)

Section 1: All persons born or naturalized in the United States…are citizens of the United States and of the State wherein they reside. No State shall make or enforce any law which shall abridge the privileges or immunities of citizens of the United States…

THE FIFTEENTH AMENDMENT
(Adopted 1870)

Section 1: The right of citizens of the United States to vote shall not be denied or abridged by the United States or by any State on account of race, color, or previous condition of servitude.

and agricultural college for black students. Washington advised blacks not to protest against political inequality but to educate themselves for manual jobs. In this way, he thought, they would slowly improve their place in society. For many black people, this simply was not enough.

A more radical approach was adopted by black sociologist WEB Du Bois. In 1905, he arranged a meeting of like-minded people near Niagara Falls, Canada. There they founded the Niagara Movement, whose aim was to win equal civil rights for blacks. It achieved little, but five years later a more effective organization, the National Association for the Advancement of Colored People (NAACP), was formed. Du Bois served as its publicity director and edited its journal, *The Crisis*.

NAACP strategy was to take to court any state government that it believed was violating the Fourteenth and Fifteenth Amendment rights of black people. Among its first victories was the 1915 *Guinn v. United States* ruling, which outlawed Oklahoma's grandfather clause. Another organization often supported the

American educator Booker T. Washington was born a slave.

NAACP in its legal battles. This was the National Urban League (NUL), founded in 1911. Its aim was to help the many southern blacks who migrated to northern cities looking for work, especially during the First World War and the Depression era.

THE SECOND WORLD WAR AND AFTER

During the Second World War, thousands more black people moved north to work in factories. They won an important legal victory in June 1941, when President Franklin D. Roosevelt issued an Executive Order establishing a Fair Employment Practices Committee (FEPC) and outlawing discrimination in defence industries. But blacks in the armed forces faced prejudice and, in the army and airforce, segregation (see page 14).

In 1942, black people set up a new civil rights organization, the Congress of Racial Equality (CORE). Founded in Chicago, its main aim was to organize protests against segregation in northern cities of the USA.

After the war ended, in 1945, the NAACP, the NUL and CORE all continued their work. It was a case brought by the NAACP that led to the historic *Brown v. Board of Education of Topeka* ruling in 1954 (see page 19). This effectively overruled the *Plessy v. Ferguson* decision and opened the way for Martin Luther King's new challenge to Jim Crow.

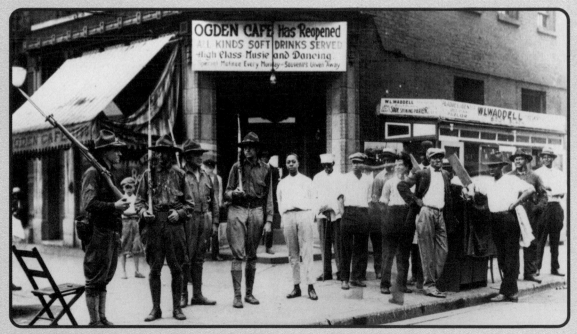

National Guardsmen patrol Chicago streets during a 1919 race riot.

CHAPTER THREE

MINISTRY IN MONTGOMERY

Soon after his marriage, King decided that he would like to take on a paying job while continuing his Ph.D. thesis in his own time. However, he was unsure whether to seek work as a college lecturer, as several of his teachers urged him to do, or to fulfil his father's dream and become a full-time Baptist preacher. Eventually, he made up his mind. He would serve as a preacher first and return to academic life later in his career.

THE MOVE TO MONTGOMERY

Early in 1954, King made his way to Montgomery, capital of the southern state of Alabama, to preach a trial sermon at Dexter Avenue Baptist Church. It was the best-known place of black Christian worship in the city, and its congregation wanted a chance to see whether this young man fresh from college would make a suitable pastor.

The 25-year-old King was nervous. Dexter's middle-class parishioners were famous for letting a man know if his sermons were not up to scratch. So he simply entrusted himself to God, and let his incomparable voice soar out over the pews, speaking about the impor-tance of leading a balanced, loving Christian life. King's fears proved groundless. At the end of the sermon, a church deacon spoke for the whole congregation when he declared: 'That did it!'

In March the same year, King was formally offered the job as Dexter's pastor. But his pleasure was combined with anxiety. He and Coretta had grown used to life in the North, and the thought of returning to the segre-gated South was not appealing. On the other hand, both had families in the region who would provide support, and King felt that it was his Christian duty to serve the black

King outside Dexter Avenue Church. The Alabama State Capitol is visible behind him.

BROWN V. BOARD OF EDUCATION OF TOPEKA

In 1954, the parents of a black girl called Linda Brown, backed by the NAACP, took the Board of Education from the town of Topeka, Kansas to court. They claimed it had no right to enforce school segregation, as the practice violated the Fourteenth Amendment to the Constitution (see page 16). The Supreme Court agreed, Chief Justice Earl Warren declaring that 'separate educational facilities are inherently unequal' and that they were likely to produce 'a feeling of inferiority' in black pupils. Every state was therefore obliged to desegregate its schools. However, the Court did not draw up a timetable for change, simply stating, in 1955, that it should go ahead 'with all deliberate speed'. Ten years later, less than 25 per cent of southern school districts had complied.

community where the need was greatest. It was a hard decision, but he began work at Dexter in May 1954, and was officially installed on 31 December.

King's new life proved testing from the outset. As well as busying himself with the usual tasks of a Christian minister – sermon-writing, religious teaching and pastoral care of parishioners – he was also active in the local chapter of the NAACP (see page 17). His thesis had to be completed, too. The only way to cope was to get up at 5.30 every day.

GROWING TENSIONS

Out in the wider world, developments were taking place that would soon lead to far greater demands on King's time. In a 1954 test case, the US Supreme Court had ruled

The large, airy interior of Dexter Avenue Baptist Church in Montgomery, Alabama. The church is still a thriving place of worship today.

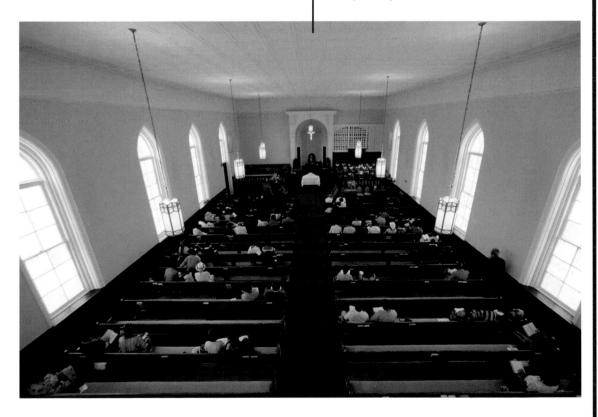

that segregated schooling was wrong and should be ended (see box on page 19). Predictably, this judgement had caused outrage throughout the South. Montgomery's 70,000 whites were used to keeping the city's 50,000 blacks in their place. So they established a White Citizens' Council to fight tooth and nail against desegregation and any other moves attempting to improve the status of the black population.

Throughout 1955, King felt the growing tension. However, he continued his daily round of work and family life largely as normal. For him, the year up to December had two highlights. In June, he was awarded his Ph.D., and in November his first child, Yolanda, was born. Known fondly as Yoki, she brought great joy to both her parents.

ROSA PARKS

Rosa Parks was a black woman employed as a seamstress in a Montgomery store. She was

Coretta King with all four of her children in 1964. Yoki is standing on the far right, next to her brother, Marty (see page 25).

also an active member of the local NAACP (see page 17). On 1 December 1955, she worked hard all day, then went Christmas shopping. When the bus came to take her home, she sat in the black section at the back, glad to rest her aching feet. But an incident then occurred that was to alter the course of the black civil rights movement in the USA. When a white man got on the now full bus, Mrs Parks refused to give up her place so that he could sit down.

Rosa Parks' action was against Montgomery law, so she was duly arrested. Once at the police station, she phoned Edward D. Nixon, a forceful NAACP official who had long sought a chance to take the city government to court about its discriminatory bus regulations. This episode seemed to be the answer to his prayers. He rushed to the station to get Mrs. Parks out on bail, then carefully began to make his plans.

THE BUS BOYCOTT

Next morning, Friday 2 December, Nixon phoned King. He explained the situation, then asked the young minister to support his idea of a bus boycott. If they could persuade Montgomery's black people not to use the city buses, Nixon argued, they could make a non-violent stand against the treatment of Rosa Parks and discrimination in general. King agreed and offered to hold a meeting of local black leaders at his church that night. There they would be able to discuss exactly how to proceed.

The meeting was held, plans were made, and 40,000 publicity leaflets printed and distributed. Then, on Sunday, black preachers across the city announced to their congregations that a bus boycott would begin the next day. After all the preparations were over, Nixon, King and fellow activists such as Ralph Abernathy, minister of Montgomery's First Baptist Church, could only wait for the morning. Would the black community respond to their call?

Rosa Lee Parks with her attorney (lawyer) Charles D. Langford in 1956, when she was arrested for participating in the bus boycott.

To their great relief, the boycott was almost total. On that Monday, Montgomery's blacks made their way to work, school and college on foot, by taxi, or in any other way that did not involve catching a bus. In court the same day, Rosa Parks was found guilty and fined the sum of $14.

THE MONTGOMERY IMPROVEMENT ASSOCIATION

Change was in the air and the black community was ready to act, but it needed clear direction. So that afternoon, King, Abernathy, Nixon and others met to discuss the right way forward. They decided to set up a body

called the Montgomery Improvement Association (MIA). It would continue to lead the boycott, and campaign more generally against racial discrimination. To his surprise, King was elected president. He was flattered, but wondered how he would deal with this extra burden.

After returning home to tell Coretta what had happened, King rushed out again to address an evening meeting at Holt Street Baptist Church. As the people in the overflowing sanctuary and the television cameras looked on, he made his first, spellbinding, public speech. King acknowledged the plight of his listeners, saying: 'You know my friends there comes a time when people get *tired* of being trampled over by the iron feet of oppression.' He accepted, too, their absolute right to protest for the equality guaranteed

21

them by the Constitution. But he also affirmed that they must protest as Christians, with love and without violence.

The crowd greeted these words with heartfelt cheers and applause, and King firmly believed God had spoken through him that night. While he recovered, shaking, from his efforts, Abernathy dealt with the down-to-earth business. The boycott, he announced, would continue until passengers, whatever their colour, were allowed to sit down on a first-come, first-served basis, until the abuse of black passengers ended, and until some black bus drivers were appointed.

CONTINUING THE STRUGGLE

These demands were extremely moderate – the MIA was not even asking for an end to bus segregation. The city authorities and bus company lawyers refused to budge, however. They were sure the boycott would soon fizzle out. But they were wrong. Day after day, thousands of Montgomery's blacks trudged to their destinations. Others used the car pool set up by the MIA. This involved making their way to pick-up points where volunteer drivers collected them and took them to work. When it was time to go home, the operation was carried out in reverse.

As 1956 arrived and the boycott continued, city leaders began to work actively against the MIA. They made it hard for the car pool to operate by refusing to renew insurance for its vehicles. They also arrested pool drivers for minor traffic offences and cancelled their licences. King was arrested for driving just over the speed limit. The usual punishment would have been a fine, but he was jailed in the police station. He was released after a crowd demonstrated outside.

UNDER THREAT

King and his family soon had to face far worse. They regularly received abusive letters and telephone calls from opponents, but were usually able to ignore them. But one

The white backlash against the 1954 Supreme Court ruling (see page 19) was severe. In Mississippi, 14-year-old Emmet Till, a summer visitor from Chicago, was murdered for speaking to a white woman.

particular call in January was especially chilling. The speaker told King to leave Montgomery within three days or 'we gonna blow your brains out and blow up your house'. King's first instinct was to do as the caller asked. How could he risk the lives of his wife and daughter? But then he felt as never before the sense that Jesus was with him, urging him onwards. There could be no turning back.

The caller's message was not an idle threat. On 30 January, while King was at a meeting, a bomb exploded on his house porch. Once he heard the news, he rushed home to see if Coretta and Yoki were all right. To his relief they were unharmed, although deeply shocked. Struggling against his anger, he resolved again to continue the fight.

THE MIRACLE OF MONTGOMERY

The boycott dragged on through 1956, and many blacks, including King, were convicted for participating. Behind the scenes, however, the MIA was making progress. In February, it had made an appeal to the federal (national) courts, claiming that bus segregation violated the Fourteenth Amendment to the Constitution (see page 16). MIA's hope was that, although the Alabama courts had continually denied blacks justice, the federal system would rule in its favour.

For much of the year, as the legal wrangling continued, King toured the USA. In this way, he won publicity for his cause and both dear friends and bitter enemies for himself. By the autumn, when he returned to Montgomery, he was exhausted. Then, in October, the city authorities tried to outlaw MIA's car pool by declaring it a 'public nuisance'. King feared he would have no choice but to end the boycott. But on 13 November 1956, the US Supreme Court announced its ruling, firmly declaring Alabama's bus segregation laws to be unconstitutional.

On 20 December 1956, 381 days after the bus boycott had begun, the historic court ruling became law in Montgomery. The following morning, King and his associates delightedly took the first unsegregated ride around the city. Despite some severe outbreaks of violence – Ralph Abernathy's house and church were bombed in January 1957, for example – the sight of blacks and whites riding the buses together soon became commonplace. The 'miracle of Montgomery' had come to pass.

Following the bus boycott victory, King is legally able to take his seat next to Glenn Smiley, a minister and supporter who taught him how to use non-violent tactics.

CHAPTER FOUR

CONTINUING THE STRUGGLE

*E*vents in Montgomery had brought King nationwide fame, as well as the respect of thousands of Americans, both black and white. But he was a humble man, who did not dwell on success. Instead he turned his attention to the even greater struggle for equality that lay ahead.

THE 1957 CIVIL RIGHTS ACT

On 17 May 1957, King took part in a prayer pilgrimage to Washington D.C., where he addressed his fellow black pilgrims on the subject of voting rights. The Fifteenth Amendment to the Constitution had given all black men the right to vote (see page 16). This was later extended to women. But by a variety of means, including the introduction of literacy tests that blacks did not have the education to pass, and poll taxes they did not have the money to pay, many state governments had effectively removed it. Now, King declared, was the time to claim it back.

Dwight D. Eisenhower, US President from 1952, had not been a great champion of the black cause, but his administration had put a piece of civil rights legislation before Congress. Following opposition from southern members, a diluted version became law in August 1957. The 1957 Civil Rights Act committed the federal government to 'securing and protecting' the black right to vote. It also established a Civil Rights Commission to investigate cases in which voter registration was blocked.

From the steps of the memorial to Abraham Lincoln, King addresses the crowd at the end of the Washington Prayer Pilgrimage.

CRISIS IN LITTLE ROCK

The urgent need to resolve the school segregation issue became abundantly clear in 1957. In the autumn of that year, nine black students tried to enrol in Central High School, a segregated establishment in Little Rock, Arkansas (see map page 9). Although they had a perfect right to do so, the state governor, Orval Faubus, called in the National Guard to prevent them. A federal court quickly ordered Faubus to remove the guards, allowing the students to enter the school. However, a 500-strong white mob then went on the rampage outside.

Eventually, President Eisenhower had to send in US army paratroopers to restore order and to protect the nine students for the rest of the school year (see right). By the autumn of 1958, when enrolment was due to begin again, Faubus had shut down the school. It did not reopen until late in 1959. King hoped that the whole frightening yet somehow ridiculous episode would encourage nationwide debate of the schools question, and so put pressure on Southerners to change their racist ways.

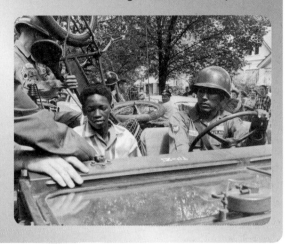

THE SCLC

The act greatly disappointed King. The voting rights measure was vague and had no time limit, while a measure allowing the federal government to enforce schools desegregation had been totally removed. In August, therefore, he invited 115 black leaders to Montgomery to plan a civil rights strategy for the coming years. Together they set up the Southern Christian Leadership Conference (SCLC), with King as president. King's responsibilities increased still further in October when his second child, Martin Luther King III ('Marty'), was born.

A NEAR MISS

The pace did not slow in 1958. In the early months of the year, two particular enterprises occupied much of King's time. The first was a book about the bus boycott, which he completed with the help of Bayard Rustin, a member of CORE (see page 17), in May. The second was the Crusade for Citizenship, an SCLC operation launched in February. Its aim was greatly to increase the number of black people registered to vote in the South. The early results, however, were disappointing.

King's book was published in September 1958. Called *Stride Toward Freedom: The Montgomery Story*, it was highly praised by many reviewers. As part of a promotional tour, King visited New York. While he was in Blumstein's department store signing copies of the book, a black woman approached him and stabbed a letter opener into his chest.

In the uproar that followed, King had the sense not to remove the blade, since that would have increased the bleeding. Instead he waited until an ambulance arrived to take him to Harlem Hospital. There, surgeons took out the weapon, later telling King that if it had been even a little closer to his aorta (heart artery), he would have died. The police soon discovered that the would-be assassin, Izola Curry, was mentally ill. At King's insistence, she was sent to hospital not jail.

25

King with his mother (left) and wife in Harlem Hospital, after an attack made in a New York store (see page 25).

During the last months of 1958, King had little choice but to rest. Then, in February 1959, he and Coretta visited India to see the places where Gandhi (see page 13) had once lived and worked. King was horrified by the squalor that he witnessed, but also impressed by government efforts to improve the lives of the poor. Returning home, he recommitted

Martin and Coretta King with Indian Prime Minister Jawaharlal Nehru, whom they met when they visited his country in early 1959.

himself to his own struggle, and to the non-violent principles he shared with Gandhi.

RETURN TO ATLANTA

King was soon back in the thick of the voting rights campaign. But he was now intent on broadening the SCLC's work. Progress towards the desegregation of schools and other public facilities remained slow, and was likely to remain so unless pressure was applied to state and federal governments. But King's plan had a major flaw. The SCLC was based in Atlanta, Georgia. But its president and guiding light, King himself, was a full-time minister in Montgomery, Alabama.

Eventually, King came to a decision – he would have to return to Atlanta so that he could devote himself more fully to the civil rights cause. But he did not intend to give up the Christian ministry completely. Instead he would preach part-time at his father's Ebenezer Baptist Church. King and his family left Dexter Avenue in January 1960. It was a sorrowful parting but one which he knew was necessary.

STUDENTS AND SIT-INS

As the King family were settling into their new Atlanta home, another development in the civil rights struggle occurred. On 1 February 1960, four black students from the North Carolina Agricultural and Technical College sat down at a lunch counter in a Woolworth's store in the town of Greensboro. This eating place was for whites only, so the students were ignored. But instead of leaving, they stayed and insisted on service.

There were sit-ins at the same Woolworth's counter for the rest of the week, the number of students involved growing daily. This simple yet effective tactic for opposing seg-regation was quickly and widely copied else-where, too. For example, some five hundred students besieged a variety of restaurants in Nashville, Tennessee, singing the protest anthem 'We Shall Overcome' as they did so.

The 1960 Woolworth's lunch counter sit-in. Other civil rights campaigners staged swimming pool 'wade-ins' and church 'pray-ins'.

SNCC

King watched this new movement with approval. He was glad students had joined the struggle and happy to give them advice when asked, always stressing the importance of non-violence. Then, in April, King attended a student conference at Shaw University, North Carolina. As well as giving the keynote speech, he urged participants to form an organization to co-ordinate student protests on different campuses.

Later that month, after discussing the idea, the students acted on King's advice and set up the Student Non-Violent Co-ordinating Committee (SNCC – pronounced 'snick'). King had thought that it might become part of the SCLC. But although the two groups shared many ideals, SNCC chose to be independent.

HARD LABOUR

In October 1960, King became more directly involved in the student movement. Since

the beginning of the autumn term, young black men and women from Atlanta colleges had been staging anti-segregation protests. Eventually, they persuaded King to join them at a sit-in. The venue was Rich's, a snack bar in a city department store. Before long, the participants were arrested for trespassing and taken to jail.

At first it seemed all might be well. Atlanta's mayor promised to help desegregate eating places and released the students. But King was tried for a minor traffic offence he had committed in a neighbouring county long before, then sentenced to four months' hard labour. Worse still, he was moved to the notoriously harsh Reidsville Penitentiary. But then, after just two days, King was mysteriously released on bail.

The mystery was soon solved. A presidential election was due in November 1960, and King had already met the Democratic Party candidate, Senator John F. Kennedy. It was this man, together with his brother and campaign manager Robert Kennedy, who had secured King's release. He quickly went on to win the election, and King fervently hoped that the new president would prove a far stronger advocate of civil rights than his fence-sitting predecessor Eisenhower.

KING AND KENNEDY

Kennedy was inaugurated in January 1961, the same month that King's third child, a boy named Dexter, was born. However, the President did not immediately make plans for new civil rights legislation, fearing this would only stir up southern opposition in Congress. Instead, he used his executive powers to further the cause. In particular, he ordered Robert Kennedy, now the Attorney General (chief law officer), to extend both the voting rights and school desegregation campaigns in the South.

To demonstrate his personal commitment to equality, President Kennedy also appointed many black people to top government jobs. For example, Thurgood Marshall, the NAACP lawyer who fought the Linda Brown case (see page 19), was made a judge in a New York Court of Appeals. King had hoped for more dramatic progress, however, and expressed his disappointment to President Kennedy when they met in the spring.

THE FREEDOM RIDES

Many civil rights organizations shared King's sense of disappointment. Among them was CORE (see page 17), whose members decided to take action. Back in 1946, the Supreme Court had ruled that segregation on interstate trains and buses was illegal. Then, in the 1960 *Boynton* v. *Virginia* case, it had

In early 1961, head of the FBI J. Edgar Hoover began a surveillance operation on King.

banned segregation at interstate bus and railway stations, too. Across the South, the rulings had been widely disregarded. CORE's aim was to bring this state of affairs to national attention.

CORE's chosen method was to set out on 'Freedom Rides', interstate trips from Washington D.C. to New Orleans, Louisiana on two buses. The passengers, black and white, were both to travel and disembark at terminals together, then see how local authorities reacted. The buses left the capital in May 1961. When they reached Anniston, Alabama, one vehicle was set on fire. Then, in Birmingham, Ku Klux Klan members attacked the Freedom Riders with baseball bats.

But there was worse to come. The few riders who had chosen to continue made their way to Montgomery, where they were attacked by a 1,000-strong white mob. The police were reluctant to intervene and the segregationist state governor, John Patterson, refused to call out the National Guard. When King arrived to support the protesters, the situation grew yet more tense. Finally, President Kennedy sent in 600 federal marshals to protect the Freedom Riders and restore order.

Both Kennedys were sympathetic to the black cause. But the President thought the Freedom Rides were unhelpfully inflammatory. He was also angry because they were distracting him from foreign policy clashes with the USSR.

Throughout the summer Robert struggled to stop further protests. In September, he finally persuaded the Interstate Commerce Commission to issue an order outlawing segregation on buses and in terminals once and for all. A short

When this 'Freedom Ride' bus stopped outside Anniston, Alabama in 1961, white protesters threw a fire bomb through its windows.

time afterwards, the victorious campaigners ended their rides.

THE ALBANY MOVEMENT

Another campaign soon demanded King's attention. In December 1961, he was called to Albany, Georgia, where the struggle to desegregate public facilities was in full swing. However the city leaders, backed by police chief Laurie Pritchett, were stubbornly resistant. King was reluctant to go, as SNCC, which often resented his involvement, was very active in the area. But Dr. William G. Anderson, leader of the Albany Movement, pleaded so hard he decided to make the journey.

In the event, King and the SCLC organized a huge range of marches, sit-ins and other anti-segregation protests in Albany. Pritchett, however, was too wily to beat black protesters in full view of television cameras, knowing this would provoke federal intervention. Instead he put them all in jail – King himself spent time in prison, but was always released so that he could not attract publicity. By

August 1962, it was clear the campaign was failing, so it was ended. The poorly planned enterprise had achieved little apart from worsening tensions between the SCLC and SNCC, which was increasingly critical of King's tactics.

TROUBLE IN MISSISSIPPI

The civil rights struggle received another blow in September, when black student James Meredith tried to enrol at the all-white University of Mississippi in Oxford. The Kennedys had sent federal marshals to protect him, but he was turned away by National Guards on the orders of state governor Ross Barnett. A second enrolment attempt led to a riot in which two people were killed. Meredith was eventually able to enrol on 1 October, but only after the administration had ordered in troops.

King was appalled by this episode and partly blamed Kennedy's lack of commitment to total desegregation. The incident also stiffened his resolve. The coming year, 1963, would mark the 100th anniversary of the Emancipation Proclamation (see page 11). Now, surely, was the time to settle the segregation issue once and for all.

CHAPTER FIVE

BIRMINGHAM AND AFTER

The Albany Movement's failure had caused King much heartache, and he longed for another chance to prove non-violent protest could work. So when, in 1963, the chance arose to launch a new campaign, he agreed. The site was to be Birmingham, Alabama, and King's main adversary the fearsome police commissioner Eugene 'Bull' Connor.

A NEW APPROACH

King and fellow SCLC members were invited to Birmingham by the Reverend Fred Shuttlesworth, head of the Alabama Christian Movement for Human Rights (ACMHR). Shuttlesworth had been trying to desegregate the city's public facilities, but had made little progress against violent opposition.

The lessons of Albany had not been wasted on King – he knew now that careful planning and selection of targets were the keys to success. So at a three-day meeting, he and the SCLC prepared their strategy in detail. First they would stage a few shop sit-ins. Then they would hold street protest marches. King knew such tactics might provoke Connor to violence. He also knew that if television pictures of this violence were broadcast, the federal government would have to act.

THE BATTLE OF BIRMINGHAM

On 28 March 1963, Coretta gave birth to the Kings' fourth child, a girl called Bernice but known as Bunny. Then, on 3 April, the Birmingham campaign began with sit-ins at five department stores. At the same time, King issued the 'Birmingham Manifesto'. It demanded the desegregation of all store facilities, the hiring of black people in local businesses, and the formation of a bi-racial committee to draw up a timetable for total desegregation. Slowly, more and more blacks joined King's operation, learned non-violent techniques and marched through the streets.

'Bull' Connor's response to the protests was to throw hundreds of the participants into jail. After King took part in a march on April 13, Good Friday, he was imprisoned, too. In solitary confinement, he read a statement about his campaign in a local newspaper. Written by eight white clergymen, it said King's protests were ill-timed and unnecessary. It urged the black community not to get involved in direct action but to fight for their cause in the courts.

King responded to this statement with his famous 'Letter from Birmingham Jail'. Writing secretly on scraps of paper, he outlined the reasons for the civil rights movement and defended his belief in non-violent direct action. He also denied the clergymen's accusation that his movement was extremist, but warned that violent separatist groups would grow if peaceful protest made no headway.

THE CHILDREN'S CRUSADE

By the time King was released from jail, on 20 April, the Birmingham campaign was fading. He and his SCLC staff decided to reinvigorate the protests by involving more black students. Younger children soon began asking to participate, too. At first, concerned these boys and girls might get hurt, King was reluctant to approve the plan. But then he realized their presence would capture the attention of the world like nothing else before.

The so-called Children's Crusade began on 2 May with a 1,000-strong march through Birmingham. As usual, Connor and his men waded in to arrest hundreds of participants. The next day, a 6,000-strong march took place, and the police chief responded more harshly. First he ordered firemen to turn their hoses on demonstrators, so that powerful jets of water knocked them to the ground. Next he ordered the police to let their Alsatian dogs loose on the terrified crowds.

A police dog rips the clothing of a terrified marcher during the 1963 Birmingham Children's Crusade.

REACHING AGREEMENT

As King had predicted, television viewers who saw these attacks were outraged. Leading politicians, including President Kennedy, rushed to express their horror and to condemn the Birmingham authorities. Meanwhile, King continued the marches and Connor, failing to learn from his mistakes, continued his violent attempts to control them. Soon the city's jails were full to bursting with school-age 'criminals'.

The federal government could not let the situation continue, so Attorney General Robert Kennedy and his staff set out to break the deadlock. Eventually, they were able to arrange negotiations between Assistant Attorney General Burke Marshall, King and his team, and local business people. On 10 May an agreement was reached that met all three demands in King's manifesto. Although unrest continued for months, the city had taken a giant step away from its Jim Crow past.

KENNEDY AND CONGRESS

The events in Birmingham sparked off other protests across the USA. They also prompted President Kennedy to take action. He prepared the way with a televised speech on 11 June 1963, in which he discussed how the civil rights issue should be tackled. In doing so, he made his own view clear. 'The time has come,' he said, 'for America to remove the blight of racial discrimination and fulfill her brilliant promise.'

Birmingham and After

Just eight days later, on 19 June, Kennedy submitted a major new civil rights bill to Congress for approval. Among its most important proposals were measures to outlaw segregation in public places and to give the federal government power to enforce school desegregation. King was delighted, but knew the bill would face opposition, especially from southern senators. So he decided to keep up the pressure.

Growing opposition

In summer 1963, black people waged non-violent campaigns against discrimination in about 900 cities across the USA. Meanwhile, King toured the country giving speeches on the civil rights movement. In general, he was welcomed and applauded. But increasing numbers of blacks, including members of a militant group called the Black Muslims, were turning against his non-violent approach.

King disagreed with the violent approach of Malcolm X (below right) to the civil rights struggle but described him as a 'sweet spirit'.

King's most outspoken black opponent during this period was Malcolm X (see page 48). A young, charismatic Black Muslim, he was regularly interviewed by journalists and always fiercely proclaimed that self-restraint would never produce equality for blacks. Instead, he claimed, black people should not hesitate to use violence against whites, and should also establish a separate black state. Malcolm X denounced Martin Luther King himself as 'a little black mouse sitting on top of a big white elephant'.

The March on Washington

Despite these challenges, King forged ahead with the campaign to pressurize Congress. The centrepiece was to be a huge march in Washington D.C., organized by himself and other prominent black activists. Many people were against the demonstration, fearing it would only stir up opposition. But King was determined it should take place.

The date set for the March on Washington was 28 August. King was one of many civil rights leaders due to make a speech when the marchers reached the city's Lincoln Memorial. The night before he worked for hours on the text, knowing this would be a unique opportunity to address thousands of people directly, as well as television viewers across the globe. He had no intention of letting it go to waste.

The march was a great success. About 250,000 people attended and peacefully made their way past the Washington Monument to the Lincoln Memorial. Once there, they joined in prayers and listened to many speeches, spirituals and gospel songs. King meanwhile waited to make his contribution, which was to be the last of the day. Then he launched into what became the most memorable speech of his career. Towards the end, he abandoned the text he had so carefully prepared to speak with great poignancy about his dream for America's future:

> ❝ I have a dream that one day…the sons of former slaves and the sons of former slaveowners will be able to sit down together at the table of brotherhood… I have a dream that my four little children will one day live in a nation where they will not be judged by the color of their skin but by the content of their character. I have a dream today. ❞

DEATH OF A PRESIDENT

The March on Washington provided a boost to King and the civil rights movement, but was not able to wipe out opposition to Kennedy's proposed new legislation. On the contrary, a southern filibuster in the Senate blocked its path into law. While the political debates continued, tension flared in the South. On 15 September, a bomb exploded at the Sixteenth Street Baptist Church in Birmingham, killing four black girls.

On 22 November, another untimely death occurred. As his motorcade was making its way through Dallas, Texas, President Kennedy was shot in the head. He died less than an hour later. Lyndon B. Johnson, Kennedy's former Vice President, was quickly sworn in as the USA's new leader. Soon afterwards, he pledged his support for the stalled civil rights bill. King was greatly relieved.

THE 1964 CIVIL RIGHTS ACT

True to his word, President Johnson used his considerable political skills to persuade southern Democrats to end the filibuster. So on 2 July 1964, with King in attendance, he was finally able to sign the Civil Rights Act into law. Its main provisions were to make

King's historic 'I Have A Dream' speech in 1963 was heard not only in Washington, but also by millions of television viewers worldwide.

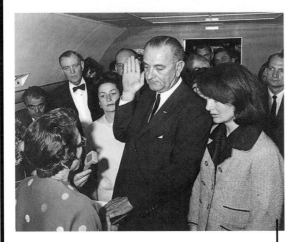

Lyndon B. Johnson is sworn in as the 36th President of the United States. Jacqueline Kennedy, widow of his assassinated predecessor, stands by his side.

King holds pictures of James Chaney, Andrew Goodman and Michael Schwerner, civil rights workers murdered during the Freedom Summer.

segregation in public places illegal, and to establish an Equal Employment Opportunity Commission (EEOC) with a mandate to fight racial discrimination in the workplace.

President Johnson and many other politicians believed that the passage of the new act would, and should, put an end to black campaigns for equality. King quickly pointed out that they were wrong. Among the difficulties still to be overcome, he asserted, was the denial of voting rights to thousands of blacks (see page 24). As usual, he did not simply define the problem, but vigorously set out to find a solution.

THE FREEDOM SUMMER

Nowhere was it more difficult for blacks to vote than in Mississippi, a poor, rural state of the Deep South. There, they were routinely intimidated by whites as they tried to register. Ku Klux Klan violence was also widespread. In mid-1964, SNCC and CORE (see page 17) began a voter registration campaign in the state. King and his SCLC colleagues also toured the area, speaking in their support.

This so-called Freedom Summer bore bitter fruit. Six civil rights workers were murdered

and over eighty injured, while fewer than 2,000 new voters were registered. Faced with this brutal reality, the campaign participants, many of them young idealists from the North, again began to question the worth of King's non-violent tactics.

PROJECT ALABAMA

Late in 1964, King learned he had won the Nobel Prize for Peace. He received the award in Norway on 10 December, then got back to business by preparing a new voting rights campaign. It was to be called Project Alabama, and its venue was to be the city of Selma in that state.

The campaign began in January 1965. As tension grew, the SCLC organized a protest march from Selma to Montgomery, the state capital. It began on Sunday 7 March, while King was in Atlanta. But after participants had walked a short way, state troopers attacked them with clubs and fired tear gas in their faces. Then local sheriff Jim Clark and his men beat them with whips. The whole, shockingly violent episode, which became known as 'Bloody Sunday', was televised nationwide.

King was horrified, and in response

arranged another march, this time of clergy from across the USA. It took place on 9 March, but ended prematurely on King's orders. SNCC criticized this decision, believing King had caved in to an assumed threat from state police. Meanwhile up in Washington, President Johnson had already decided to act.

THE 1965 VOTING RIGHTS ACT

On 15 March, in a speech to Congress, Johnson declared it was 'deadly wrong' to deny any Americans the right to vote. Then he put forward a bill proposing a radical new voting rights act. As usual, King kept up the pressure. Beginning on 21 March, he finally led a march the full 80 kilometres from Selma to Montgomery. At its end, on 25 March, he made a speech in the city where he had begun his campaigning ten years before. The watching crowd of 25,000 joyfully sang 'We *Have* Overcome'.

The 1965 Voting Rights Act eventually passed into law on 6 August 1965. It banned literacy tests and all other restrictive practices in states where under half the

In a ceremony in Oslo, Norway, King receives the Nobel Prize for Peace from Gunnar Jahn, President of the Nobel Prize Committee.

population had voted or registered to vote in 1964. It also arranged for the appointment of federal registrars, whose role was to visit southern states and ensure black people could claim their right to vote without intimidation. A major victory had been won.

SHOWDOWN IN ST AUGUSTINE

In spring 1964, before the passage of the Civil Rights Act, King received a call for help from the black community of St Augustine, Florida. This town was the oldest permanent European settlement in the USA, and its white population was resisting all efforts to end segregation. King decided it would be an ideal location for further demonstrations, so sent SCLC members to plan a campaign.

After organized action began in May, the local Ku Klux Klan responded with protests (see right) and brutality. When King arrived, he asked the President to send in federal marshals to restore order, but Johnson refused. The disturbances continued until June, when King was briefly imprisoned for requesting service in a whites-only

restaurant. Then, unexpectedly, state governor Farris Bryant set up a biracial committee to work out a solution to the town's race problems. No changes were promised, but King could rightly claim that at least some progress had been made.

CHAPTER SIX

WHERE DO WE GO FROM HERE?

Once the Civil and Voting Rights Acts had become law, King pondered what to do next. Soon he began to consider an issue that had been troubling him for some time – the situation of blacks in the North. They had not suffered official segregation like those in the South, but many thousands still lived in poor ghettos and had neither jobs nor hope for the future. Now King decided to turn his attention to their plight.

TAKING ACTION

There had been race riots in the cities of the North since the early 20th century. Several had erupted during the summer of 1964, for example in New York. But it was a riot of August 1965 that finally spurred King into action. The location was Watts, a black suburb of Los Angeles, and the trigger a policeman's attack on a member of a crowd protesting against another man's arrest. Within six days, 34 people had been killed.

King made a brief trip to Watts, but decided the first focus of his northern campaign would be Chicago. He had visited this city in July, so had seen the injustice as well as the school and housing segregation its black population faced. In addition, local black activist Reverend Jesse Jackson was already leading an effective campaign there called 'Operation Breadbasket'. It used boycotts and other tactics to persuade white owners of food shops and other businesses to hire black staff. The city was therefore an ideal site for a landmark struggle against discrimination.

KING AND VIETNAM

During this period, King had another major issue on his mind, too. The USA had been supporting non-Communist South Vietnam against Communist North Vietnam since the 1950s. But in 1965, President Lyndon Johnson had begun greatly to increase his country's

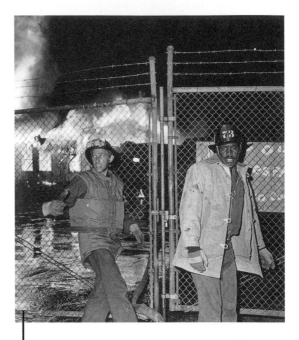

Firefighters in the Watts suburb of Los Angeles extinguished blazes in shops and other buildings during the 1965 race riot.

military involvement, sending in 50,000 extra troops and promising more.

King was dismayed by this development, not only because he believed in non-violence, but also because he thought the USA should not interfere in other countries. His criticism of American intervention brought widespread condemnation, however, from the President and some of King's own SCLC allies.

THE CHICAGO CAMPAIGN

King's Chicago campaign began in January 1966, and his first aim was to end the terrible conditions in the city's slums. Knowing this would involve taking on the powerful Mayor of Chicago, Richard J. Daley, he moved into a rat-infested slum flat in the city to be close to the action.

Mayor Daley frustrated King's efforts without resorting to abuse or violence. For example, as soon as King began to criticize housing conditions, Daley started taking slum landlords to court, forcing them to repair their tenements. He also publicized the city government's own on-going contributions to slum improvement, such as its pest control programme. His clear message was that King's intervention was unnecessary. Many Chicago residents, both black and white, agreed.

BLACK POWER

As the Chicago campaign stumbled on, there was a disturbing development in the South. In June 1966, James Meredith (see page 29) staged a one-man 'March Against Fear' from Memphis, Tennessee to Jackson, Mississippi. He aimed to show that blacks could now walk long distances without fear of attack, so should not be afraid to take the short walk to the polling station. But in Mississippi, he was shot by a white sniper.

Hearing this news, King flew to Memphis, where Meredith was in hospital. Also at his bedside were Stokely Carmichael, leader of SNCC, and Floyd McKissick, head of CORE. The three men decided to organize a joint march from where Meredith was shot to Jackson. But during the trek, they argued over non-violence and white partici-pation. King supported both, Carmichael and McKissick neither.

The conflict came to a head when Carmichael declared to a crowd in Greenwood, Mississippi that nothing had been achieved in six years of pleading for freedom, and that a new slogan was needed: Black Power (see page 49). This phrase appalled King because it seemed to hint at

In his 1964 State of the Union speech, President Johnson committed himself to the fight against poverty in the USA.

the use of violence and black separatism. Carmichael eventually agreed to ban its use until the march ended in Jackson. But after-wards, 'Black Power!' became a rallying cry for many angry blacks across the nation.

CONFRONTATION IN CHICAGO

King next made his way back to Chicago, where his family were also spending the summer. Then he began organizing a march to City Hall, the Mayor's headquarters. It took place on 10 July, and over 30,000 people participated. Once they had reached their destination, King taped a list of demands to the door. Mayor Daley, however, was not at all impressed. The next day he told King in no uncertain terms to back off.

It was a blistering hot summer and life was not pleasant for the King family in their dingy, cramped flat. Outside on the streets tensions rose, too, and many young blacks rioted night after night. Working with Mayor Daley, King managed to restore a measure of calm, then stepped up his non-violent protest campaign. Now the plan was to march through neighbourhoods where no blacks were able to live because residents and estate agents worked together to keep them out.

The marches against segregated housing stirred up some of the most vicious opposition King had ever seen. But as whites hurled rocks, the protesters remained non-violent. Eventually, Mayor Daley called King in for a meeting on 26 August and they thrashed out an agreement. It committed the city to a more just housing policy, and at first King believed he had won. In fact, however, the agreement contained neither guar-antees nor a timetable for change, and had little long-term effect.

WHERE DO WE GO FROM HERE?

WHERE DO WE GO FROM HERE?

King returned to Atlanta in autumn 1966. There he spent long hours brooding about the split in the civil rights movement between those who opposed and those who supported the use of violence. He was also depressed about the growing 'white backlash' against black gains.

King discussed these issues and more in a book he wrote early in 1967. *Where Do We Go From Here?* outlined his opposition to what he saw as the destructive aspects of the 'Black Power' movement. At the same time, it encouraged black people to continue the fight for equal treatment. King developed a new strand of thinking in the book, too. Now, he said, the struggle for justice should be widened to include other disadvantaged groups, from poor whites to Puerto Ricans.

(From left to right) King, the wounded James Meredith, Stokely Carmichael and Floyd McKissick on the 1966 march to Jackson.

OPPOSING VIETNAM

Developments in the Vietnam War also greatly troubled King at this time. Since President Johnson's original intervention (see page 36), the number of American troops in the country had risen steadily, reaching almost 500,000 in 1967. These forces had killed thousands of innocent civilians, yet still victory was not in sight.

In King's view, the war was not only evil in itself, it was costing billions of dollars that could be better spent helping the poor at home. In addition, it was sending thousands of Americans, a disproportionate number of them black, to their deaths. Feeling morally obliged to take a stand, King made numerous anti-war speeches. On 4 April, at the Riverside Church, New York, he even compared some American actions in Vietnam to those of the Nazis, and called for an immediate ceasefire.

The response was fierce. Many politicians and journalists criticized King for venturing into areas that were supposedly beyond his

THE BLACK PANTHERS

The Black Muslims (see page 32) and SNCC were not the only organizations who denounced King's non-violence. Equally if not more critical of his stance was the Black Panther party, a militant group founded by students Huey Newton and Bobby Seale in Oakland, California in 1966. Its members wore military-style uniforms and were sometimes armed. They also raised their right fists (see right) as a sign of their commitment to 'Black Power'.

competence. Others denounced him as a closet Communist who wanted the North Vietnamese to win. King also faced opposition from NAACP and other black leaders, who believed that by antagonizing President Johnson he was putting the civil rights cause at risk. However Stokely Carmichael and SNCC were glad to give him their support.

King was taken aback by the extent of the criticism. Nevertheless, he remained sure that he was right and agreed to participate in a major anti-war march in New York on 15 April. Walking alongside 125,000 other protesters, including Carmichael, he made his way from Central Park to the United Nations building, then addressed the crowd. Always a patriot, however, King carefully distanced himself from demonstrators who burned an American flag and their draft cards.

THE POOR PEOPLE'S CAMPAIGN

During the summer of 1967, King watched in horror as race riots erupted in many northern cities. The worst affected was Detroit, Michigan, where 43 people were killed in July. King's appeal to President Johnson to reduce the unemployment and poor housing conditions that fuelled such outbursts proved fruitless. So he turned again to direct action.

His new plan was highly ambitious. As he had suggested in *Where Do We Go From Here?*, he intended to draw together people from many sections of society in a Poor People's Campaign. They would march from all across the USA to Washington D.C., then begin a massive protest programme. And they would not leave after a day, but camp out in city parks. At the same time, King would demand that the government introduce a Bill of Rights for the Disadvantaged.

Even before King officially launched the Poor People's Campaign in December 1967, many people had voiced opposition. They included some black leaders who feared the demonstrations would soon descend into violence. After the plans were made public, antagonism came from many more quarters. President Johnson, who believed he had already done enough for poor blacks, considered the campaign a personal insult. He was also afraid it might bring chaos to the American capital.

Despite all the criticism, King went ahead. His plan was that protesters should reach Washington in spring 1968, so he spent the New Year frantically making preparations. The pressure took its toll, leaving him tired and depressed. His anxiety was not only about the future of the movement, but also his own fate. He had been receiving assassination threats for years. But now they played on his mind as never before.

WHERE DO WE GO FROM HERE?

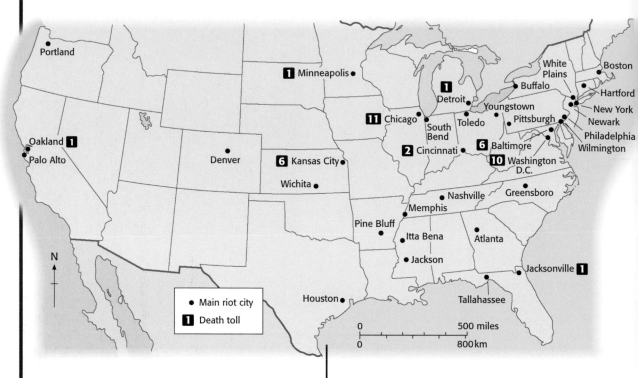

MAYHEM IN MEMPHIS

In February 1968, 1,300 rubbish collectors from Memphis, Tennessee, went on strike because the city government had refused to increase their pay, improve their working conditions or recognize their union. As 90 per cent of the workers were black, they appealed to James Lawson, SCLC member and pastor of the Centenary Methodist Church, for help.

Lawson in his turn asked King for support. He agreed, first addressing a rally in Memphis on 18 March, then flying back in to lead a protest march ten days later. On arrival, King made his way to the Clayborn Temple, stationed himself at the head of the crowds gathered there and started walking into the city centre. Shortly after, members of a local black group called 'The Invaders' began breaking shop windows and stealing the goods inside. As soon as he became aware of the violence, King stopped the march.

It was too late to prevent a riot. By its end, a black boy was dead and 80 other people were wounded. The whole episode aroused

This map shows the main American cities where riots broke out after the death of King in 1968. A total of 168 cities were affected.

more hostility against King. If he could not control these protesters, people said, how could he claim there would be no violence in Washington?

A TRAGIC END

Thinking the matter over back in Atlanta, King now decided that the only way to demonstrate his commitment to non-violence was to return to Memphis once more. So he called another march for 5 April.

King arrived back in the city on 3 April with his trusted colleague Ralph Abernathy (see page 20) by his side. After checking in to the Lorraine Motel, the two men busied themselves with preparations for the march. In the evening, King delivered a heart-stopping speech at the Mason Temple. Reviewing his life, he thanked God he had not died when he was stabbed in 1958 (see page 25). Then he went on:

40

King on the balcony of the Lorraine Motel in Memphis where he was shot. To his left is Jesse Jackson and to his right Ralph Abernathy.

A grief-stricken Coretta King at her husband's funeral. She worked to preserve his memory until her death in 2006.

'We've got some difficult days ahead. But it really doesn't matter with me now. Because I've been to the mountaintop… And I've looked over. And I've seen the Promised Land. And I may not get there with you. But I want you to know tonight that we as a people *will* get to the Promised Land.'

The next day, Thursday 4 April 1968, King and his team were due to have dinner at the house of local black pastor Samuel Kyles. He came to collect them some time after half past five, but as they were about to leave, Abernathy asked King to wait while he put on some aftershave lotion. King then stepped out on to the balcony of his motel room and chatted to his other friends, who were already in the car park below.

The next second, a shot rang out. It hit King on the right side of the face, doing terrible damage. At once Abernathy came to his aid and an ambulance was called. But King was beyond help, and died in St Joseph's Hospital, Memphis at just after seven o'clock. He was buried in Atlanta on 8 April while over 50,000 mourners, including his beloved wife and children, looked on. A white man called James Earl Ray, who had been in and out of prison all his life, was convicted of his murder.

PREACHER OR POLITICIAN?

Martin Luther King began his working life as a Baptist pastor and continued to preach throughout his career. Nevertheless, in 1960 he abandoned full-time ministry to devote himself to the struggle for black civil rights. In this role, for which he is chiefly remembered, King developed impressive political skills. In the courts and on the streets, quoting the Constitution as well as the Bible, he took on the American establishment and won major victories. So was King a political preacher, a religious politician or a mixture of the two? Read both sides of the argument and the sources below, then judge for yourself.

PREACHER?

SOURCE 1

This is my being and my heritage for I am also the son of a Baptist preacher, the grandson of a Baptist preacher and the great-grandson of a Baptist preacher.
(MARTIN LUTHER KING)

SOURCE 2

'I came to see that God had placed a responsibility on my shoulders and the more I tried to escape it, the more frustrated I would become.'
(MARTIN LUTHER KING)

SOURCE 3

The teachings of the Great Three – Jesus, Thoreau, and Gandhi – have been brought together…The new synthesis is known simply as a 'philosophy of love'… an alternative to the conflict and killing that we usually associate with social progress.
(EXTRACT FROM *CRUSADER WITHOUT VIOLENCE* BY L.D. REDDICK)

A PREACHING TRADITION

Martin Luther King was born into a long line of Baptist preachers (*Source 1*). He grew up strongly aware of this rich tradition, which was reinforced every time he heard his father address the black congregation at Atlanta's Ebenezer Baptist Church. King also learned early that a preaching vocation did not mean a man need concern himself only with the afterlife. His father worked tirelessly to help black people on Earth.

King preaching at Ebenezer Baptist Church, Atlanta.

FROM DOUBT TO FAITH

In his early teenage years, King rebelled against his father's clear expectation that he, too, would be a preacher. Not only did he doubt the truth of Christianity, but he also began to think there were better ways to serve the black community. However, at Morehouse College he learned a more liberal form of Christianity that he could accept (see page 8). By 17, he was committed to becoming a minister (*Source 2*).

A NEW PHILOSOPHY

After King was ordained in 1948 (see page 9), he divided his time between continuing his education and preaching. All the while, at both Crozer and Boston, he read widely:

from the Bible, of course, but also from the works of Gandhi (see page 13) and many others. By 1954, when he began his ministry at Dexter Baptist Church in Montgomery, he had devised a philosophy that combined many ideals (*Source 3*). But at its heart was the deeply Christian notion that ordinary believers might have to suffer as Jesus had done in order to change the world for the better.

MONTGOMERY AND AFTER

During his five-and-a-half years in Montgomery, King acquired a reputation as a skilful preacher, whose oratory could inspire both the illiterate and the educated. Such was his fame that he was invited to give sermons in many other churches. It was also during this period that he first experienced the sense that God was speaking through him (see page 22). Even after 1960, when King left to work for the SCLC in Atlanta (see page 26), he did not give up preaching. On the contrary, he again became, and always remained, co-pastor at his father's church.

PREACHING WITHOUT A PULPIT

Once he began his civil rights work in earnest, King used his preaching gift to influence a far wider audience. Whether at small, local meetings or major rallies such as the 1963 March on Washington (see page 32), he employed ringing phrases, heartfelt pleas and mesmerizing repetition to drive his message home. Often black audiences would respond aloud, just as though in church (*Source 4*). In other words, King's 'political' speeches were really a form of preaching without a pulpit (*Source 5*).

A PREACHER AT HEART

King spent most of his adult life struggling to win economic and political rights for the black people of the USA. But he did so as a preacher, not a politician (*Source 6*). He was never interested in gaining power for himself, but in using his talents, and if necessary suffering, to convey his faith and to turn his dreams of a better future into reality.

King at a service for James Reeb, a pastor killed at Selma.

SOURCE 4

I come to tell you tonight in Selma, you may not have a lot of money (No), you may not have degrees surrounding your name…; you may not know all the intricacies of the English language (No); you may not have your grammar right (Right); but I want you to know that you are as good as any Ph.D in English (shouts and applause). I come to Selma to say to you tonight that, oh, (Speak! speak!) that you are God's children and therefore you are some-body (tumult).
(KING SPEAKING IN SELMA IN 1965. THE WORDS IN BRACKETS ARE THE AUDIENCE RESPONSE)

SOURCE 5

The substance of [his] sermons he translated into civil religious addresses and fiery mass-meeting speeches, but it was always preaching that he was doing. Even when no [Bible] text was cited and the deity [God] was not mentioned, the audiences to these speeches considered themselves no less a congregation.
(EXTRACT FROM *THE PREACHER KING, MARTIN LUTHER KING, JR. AND THE WORD THAT MOVED AMERICA* BY RICHARD LISCHER)

SOURCE 6

In the quiet recesses of my heart, I am fundamentally a clergyman, a Baptist preacher.
(MARTIN LUTHER KING)

PREACHER OR POLITICIAN?

POLITICIAN?

SOURCE 7

I have passed spots where Negroes had been savagely lynched...I had seen police brutality with my own eyes and watched Negroes receive the most tragic injustices in the courts.
(EXTRACT FROM STRIDE TOWARD FREEDOM BY MARTIN LUTHER KING)

SOURCE 8

Unjust laws exist: shall we be content then to obey them, or shall we endeavour to amend them, and obey them until we have succeeded, or shall we transgress [break] them at once? Men generally... think that, if they should resist, the remedy would be worse than the evil. But why does it [the government] not encourage its citizens to be on the alert to point out its faults...?
(EXTRACT FROM CIVIL DISOBEDIENCE (1849) BY HENRY DAVID THOREAU)

SOURCE 9

I was so deeply moved that I reread the [Thoreau's] work several times. This was my first intellectual contact with the theory of nonviolence and resistance.
(EXTRACT FROM STRIDE TOWARD FREEDOM BY MARTIN LUTHER KING)

WORKING FOR CHANGE

There is no doubt that in all he did, King was inspired by his Christian faith. He also had the training and instincts of a preacher. Nevertheless, once he left full-time ministry in 1960, he had to become a politician in order to succeed in his chosen task. This does not mean that he joined a party or stood for election. Rather he engaged in politics in its broadest sense of activities designed to produce social and economic change.

King at the White House in 1963, where he met President Kennedy (fourth from the right).

EARLY INFLUENCES

From a young age, King was shocked at the injustice black Americans suffered (*Source 7*), and at the government's failure to help them. His reading of Thoreau while at Morehouse College (see page 8) introduced him to the idea of resisting such institutionalized prejudice using non-violent means (*Sources 8* and *9*). King's later discovery of Gandhi's works (see page 13) strengthened his new ideals. In them, he saw how a religious man could engage fully in a political struggle for the sake of his people.

THE MONTGOMERY MINISTRY

Until King became minister of Dexter Baptist in 1954, he had no opportunity to put his ideals into practice. But then he quickly set up a programme to help the poor and became a member of the local NAACP committee. King's subsequent handling of the bus boycott and election as MIA president (see page 21) were clear early signs of his political skills. Already in his speech at Holt Street Church (see page 21), he was basing arguments on political as well as religious texts (*Source 10*).

A NEW ROLE

After setting up the SCLC in 1957, King engaged in more political struggles that took him away from church work. By 1960, he could no longer combine the roles of preacher and politician, so he chose the latter (*Source 11*). Soon after he began working for the SCLC full-time, SNCC sit-ins and CORE 'Freedom Rides' took place (see page 28). The participants forced the government to act by provoking their opponents to violence. It was a lesson that King the politician quickly learned.

POLITICAL TALENTS

During the major campaigns that followed, King used his political talents to great effect. Not only did he mastermind demonstrations, he also dealt skilfully with the authorities at every level. In Birmingham, for example (see page 30), King openly defied police chief Eugene 'Bull' Connor, knowing he would respond with violence and so earn condemnation. When meeting Presidents Kennedy and Johnson, by contrast, King used reasoned argument to make his case. But he was never afraid to oppose presidential policy, and spoke out in particular against Johnson's intervention in Vietnam (see page 36).

Coretta King celebrates Martin Luther King day, a national holiday to mark King's political achievements (see page 59).

PRACTICAL POLITICIAN

King was a deeply religious man. But it was his political skills, and his willingness to engage in political struggle, that distinguished him from other black leaders. Without these qualities, he would never have won freedom for his people and a place in history for himself (*Source 12*).

SOURCE 10

If we are wrong, the Supreme Court of this nation is wrong. If we are wrong, the Constitution of the United States is wrong. If we are wrong, God Almighty is wrong. If we are wrong, Jesus of Nazareth is merely a Utopian dreamer who never came down to Earth.
(MARTIN LUTHER KING IN HIS SPEECH ABOUT THE BUS BOYCOTT AT MONTGOMERY'S HOLT STREET BAPTIST CHURCH, 5 DECEMBER 1955)

SOURCE 11

History was calling him home to Atlanta, obliging him to abandon his role as a preacher with a concern for civil rights and become a militant movement leader with a private and abiding religious faith.
(EXTRACT FROM LET THE TRUMPET SOUND, A LIFE OF MARTIN LUTHER KING BY STEPHEN B. OATES)

SOURCE 12

Martin Luther King, Jr., was the conscience of his generation. A Southerner, a black man, he gazed upon the great wall of segregation and saw that the power of love could bring it down.
(EXTRACT FROM THE CITATION ACCOMPANYING THE AWARD OF THE PRESIDENTIAL MEDAL OF FREEDOM TO KING ON 4 JULY 1977)

NON-VIOLENCE – EFFECTIVE OR NAIVE?

Martin Luther King began to formulate his philosophy of non-violence during his college years. Later, as a civil rights leader, he claimed it was the only way to bring about reform that was both practical and moral. But during the 1960s, SNCC and other, more radical groups questioned King's methods. They maintained that violence was a legitimate response to the discrimination and cruelty encountered by blacks. So was non-violence the most effective way to secure change, as King believed, or was it simply a naive policy of only limited usefulness? Read both sides of the argument and the sources below, then judge for yourself.

EFFECTIVE?

SOURCE 1

Love your enemies, do good to those who hate you, bless those who curse you, pray for those who ill-treat you. If someone strikes you on one cheek, turn to him the other also.
(JESUS CHRIST, AS QUOTED IN THE GOSPEL OF LUKE, CHAPTER 6, VERSES 27–29)

SOURCE 2

I found that the term 'passive resistance' was too narrowly construed [understood], *that it was supposed to be a weapon of the weak, that it could be characterized by hatred, and that it could finally manifest itself as violence, I had to…explain the real nature of the movement… Maganlal Gandhi coined the word 'Sadagraha'…But in order to make it clearer I changed the word to 'Satyagraha'* [Sadagraha means 'firmness in a good cause', Satyagraha means 'truth force'].
(EXTRACT FROM *AN AUTOBIOGRAPHY* BY M.K. GANDHI)

A NEW APPROACH

As a teenager, King thought non-violence a weak creed that could not defeat evil. The teachings of Jesus (*Source 1*) and Thoreau (see page 9) helped to change his mind. But it was through reading Gandhi's autobiography that King realized passive resistance (non-violence) was a form of strength (*Source 2*) and a way of overcoming injustice (*Source 3*).

THE MONTGOMERY MIRACLE

King preached non-violence throughout the 1955–56 Montgomery bus boycott, explicitly ruling out the murderous tactics favoured by the Ku Klux Klan (*Source 4*). The willingness of blacks to follow his lead, and the success of the boycott, proved that non-violent methods could work. King argued this point firmly in his 1958 book *Stride Toward Freedom*.

Students at a workshop learn how to remain non-violent despite provocation.

PROVOCATION AND PUBLICITY

King's 1959 trip to India strengthened his commitment to Gandhi's way of non-violence. Back home, he slowly increased his understanding of how best to follow it. The Freedom Rides taught him many lessons. He learned in particular that non-violent provocation of violence and the staging of 'theatrical' events brought to the surface the brutality underpinning discrimination and provided vital publicity (*Source 5*).

ALBANY, BIRMINGHAM AND SELMA

In the 1961–62 Albany campaign, King hoped to put his new ideas into practice. However, the refusal of police chief Laurie Pritchett to use violence denied the protesters publicity and little was achieved. By contrast, during the 1963 Birmingham campaign, the brutal response of police commissioner Eugene 'Bull' Connor brought TV coverage and the intervention of President Kennedy. In 1965, events followed a similar course in Selma, where 'Bloody Sunday' caused Johnson to act.

REASONS FOR RESTRAINT

During these campaigns, King often explained some of his reasons for using non-violent tactics. He told protesters that such methods put them morally beyond reproach, while making it hard for whites to justify violent counter-measures. In addition, whenever blacks had attempted revolt, for example during slavery, white forces had crushed them. The same method, he declared, would still produce the same outcome.

The violent slave revolt led by Nat Turner in 1831 was quashed in just a few days.

KEEPING THE FAITH

When the Black Power movement emerged in 1966, King refused to abandon his principles. On the contrary, during the Chicago campaign he taught many more people the ideals and techniques of non-violence. In 1967, King's book *Where Do We Go From Here?* and his anti-Vietnam speeches reaffirmed his opposition to all violence. His tragic assassination in 1968 demonstrated just how destructive it could be.

NECESSARY NON-VIOLENCE

King believed non-violence was effective, prevented an overwhelming white backlash, and was morally right. In his view, violence would lead only to the spiritual self-destruction of its perpetrators and a bitter, divided society (*Source 6*).

SOURCE 3

King thought Gandhi one of the great men of all time. 'He was probably the first person in history to lift the love ethic of Jesus above mere interaction between individuals to a powerful effective social force on a large scale.'
(EXTRACT FROM *LET THE TRUMPET SOUND, A LIFE OF MARTIN LUTHER KING* BY STEPHEN B. OATES)

SOURCE 4

There will be no crosses burned at any bus stops in Montgomery. There will be no white persons pulled out of their homes and taken out on some distant road and murdered... We are not...advocating violence. We have overcome that.
(EXTRACT FROM KING'S SPEECH AT HOLT STREET, DECEMBER 1955)

SOURCE 5

Without the presence of the press, there might have been untold massacre in the South. The world seldom believes the horror stories of history until they are documented via mass media.
(MARTIN LUTHER KING SPEAKING ABOUT THE FREEDOM RIDES)

SOURCE 6

I am convinced that if we succumb to the temptation to use violence in our struggle for freedom, unborn generations will be the recipients of a long and desolate night of bitterness, and our chief legacy to them will be a never-ending reign of chaos.
(MARTIN LUTHER KING)

NON-VIOLENCE — EFFECTIVE OR NAIVE?

NAIVE?

SOURCE 7

There are many of my poor black ignorant brothers... preaching the ignorant and lying stuff that you should love your enemy. What fool can love his enemy?
(ELIJAH MUHAMMAD)

SOURCE 8

I don't profess to have a political, economic, or social solution to a problem as complicated as the one which our people face in the States, but I am one of those who is willing to try any means necessary to bring an end to the injustices that our people suffer.
(MALCOLM X IN BY ANY MEANS NECESSARY: SPEECHES, INTERVIEWS, AND A LETTER, BY MALCOLM X)

SOURCE 9

Well I believe it's a crime for anyone who is being brutalized to continue to accept that brutality without doing something to defend himself. If that's how 'Christian' philosophy is interpreted, if that's what Gandhian philosophy teaches, well, then, I will call them criminal philosophies...I am for violence if non-violence means we continue postponing a solution to the American black man's problem.
(EXTRACT FROM THE AUTOBIOGRAPHY OF MALCOLM X)

ADVOCATES OF VIOLENCE

Some black Americans always opposed King's doctrine of non-violence, believing it was a feeble response to injustice. But it was not until the 1960s that large numbers began openly to advocate violent tactics. For them, the Christian philosophy of loving resistance was not enough.

MALCOLM X AND THE BLACK MUSLIMS

In 1952 Malcolm X, a fiery young man who had led a wild life on the streets of Harlem, New York, joined an organization called the Nation of Islam. Its members, known as Black Muslims, believed that all black Americans were descendants of a Muslim tribe and should reject Christianity. The Nation's leader of the time, Elijah Muhammad, denounced non-violence (*Source 7*), and urged black people to found a separate state within the USA.

Malcolm X soon became the Nation of Islam's spokesman, and in that role regularly clashed with King. They disagreed especially about violence, Malcolm firmly maintaining it had a part to play in the black struggle (*Sources 8* and *9*). Malcolm X left the Nation of Islam in 1964, converted to orthodox Islam and became less hostile to whites. But he and his followers continued to believe that violence could be valid. Malcolm was shot dead by a Nation of Islam member in 1965.

Malcolm X speaking in Washington D.C. in May 1963.

SNCC

Less militant organizations turned against King's methods, too. Among them was the Student Non-Violent Co-ordinating Committee (see page 27).

Its members were originally dedicated to non-violence, but white brutality changed their views. The terrible events of the 1964 Freedom Summer in Mississippi were a major turning point (see page 34). But it was in 1966 that SNCC commitment to non-violence finally dissolved.

BLACK POWER

Even after the Civil and Voting Rights Acts, SNCC members felt little had changed. The 'Black Power' slogan their leader Stokely Carmichael coined during the 1966 March Against Fear (*Source 10*) gave them a way to express their rage. When King took his non-violent message to cities such as Chicago, SNCC and others responded with a new militancy (*Source 11*). Unsure about the worth of King's tactics in the South, they considered them inadequate for riot-torn northern ghettos.

SNCC leader Rap Brown urged blacks to move from 'resistance to aggression'.

FLAWED THEORY?

Not all campaigners opposed King's non-violence because it had failed to produce the benefits that they sought. Quoting black psychiatrist Frantz Fanon and others, some also claimed it was unhealthy for the oppressed not to strike back (*Sources 12* and *13*). Another criticism of King's approach was that it worked only when it deliberately provoked violence (see page 30), and so was not really non-violent at all.

NAIVE NON-VIOLENCE

Opponents of King's non-violent doctrine criticized it for a wide variety of reasons. Some thought it was morally wrong, some that it was ineffective, and others that it was unhealthy. But they all agreed that it was a naive response to a profoundly serious and deep-rooted problem.

SOURCE 10

The only way we gonna stop them white men from whuppin' us is to take over. We been saying freedom for six years and we ain't got nothin'. What we gonna start saying now is Black Power!
(STOKELY CARMICHAEL, 1966)

SOURCE 11

Now it is over. The days of singing freedom songs and the days of combating bullets and billy clubs with love...They used to sing "I Love Everybody" as they ducked bricks and bottles. Now they sing:
   Too much love,
   Too much love,
   Nothing kills a nigger like
   Too much love.
(SNCC MEMBER AND WRITER JULIUS LESTER. THE OFFENSIVE TERM 'NIGGER' WAS HIS)

SOURCE 12

[Violence is] *a psychologically healthy and tactically sound method for the oppressed.*
(EXTRACT FROM *THE WRETCHED OF THE EARTH* BY FRANTZ FANON)

SOURCE 13

By arguing that violence is as American as cherry pie...some have loudly advocated violence as the only appropriate means for achieving racial justice. To pretend otherwise would be equal to calling upon black men to contradict their own basic, natural, and..."healthy" tendencies.
(EXTRACT FROM *THE POLITICAL PHILOSOPHY OF MARTIN LUTHER KING JR.*, BY HANES WALTON JR.)

CIVIL RIGHTS LEGISLATION — SUCCESS OR FAILURE?

It was largely thanks to the efforts of Martin Luther King and his supporters that the 1964 Civil Rights Act and 1965 Voting Rights Act passed into law. At the time, these pieces of legislation were acclaimed as great milestones on the road to black equality. It soon became clear, however, that black Americans had many more obstacles to overcome. They included not only the difficulty of implementing the acts, but also a range of problems that lay outside their scope, such as poverty. So was the civil rights legislation of the 1960s a success or a failure? Read both sides of the argument and the sources below, then judge for yourself.

SUCCESS?

SOURCE 1

Nobody needs to convince me any longer that we have to solve the problem [of racial injustice], not let it drift...
(PRESIDENT JOHN F. KENNEDY, SPEAKING TO KING IN 1961)

SOURCE 2

REGISTRAR: What do you want?
CRAWFORD: I brought this lady down to register.
REGISTRAR:...Why did you bring this lady down here?
CRAWFORD: Because she wants to be a first class citizen like y'all.
REGISTRAR: Who are you to bring people down to register?
CRAWFORD: It's my job.
REGISTRAR: Suppose you get two bullets in your head right now?
(EXTRACT FROM A CONVERSATION BETWEEN SNCC MEMBER JAMES CRAWFORD AND A DEPUTY REGISTRAR IN LEE COUNTY, GEORGIA)

TWIN EVILS

Martin Luther King learned about the injustice of segregation as a child and continued to witness its damaging effects as he grew older. His concern with black disenfranchisement developed later, but was no less strongly felt. King spent much of his life campaigning for federal legislation to outlaw these twin evils. His efforts were not in vain.

President Eisenhower signs the 1957 Civil Rights Act.

EARLY EFFORTS

Soon after King began his work, during the Eisenhower administration, the 1957 Civil Rights Act was passed (see page 24). But it failed to end the denial of black voting rights, even after it was strengthened in 1960. When Kennedy came to power, he vowed to support King's cause (*Source 1*), but was reluctant to introduce new laws.

KENNEDY IN ACTION

Eager to change Kennedy's mind, King held many campaigns in the early 1960s, for example in Albany, Georgia (see page 29). But segregation and the widespread exclusion of blacks from the voting register persisted (*Source 2*). The violence that erupted during the 1963 protests in Birmingham finally spurred Kennedy into action (*Source 3*). He submitted a Civil Rights bill to Congress in June the same year.

THE 1964 CIVIL RIGHTS ACT

The bill became law during the Johnson administration, in July 1964 (see page 33). This new Civil Rights Act included many measures for which King had struggled, such as an end to segregation (*Source 4*) and the establishment of an Equal Employment Opportunity Commission. It also gave the federal government extra powers to speed up school desegregation and to protect black voting rights. President Johnson believed that the Act would end racial discrimination in the USA.

CLAIMING THE VOTE

King realized the 1964 Civil Rights Act had given black Americans life-changing new freedoms. However, he also thought it had deep flaws. The worst, in his view, was its failure to ban literacy tests and other tricks that whites used to stop blacks voting. By early 1965, 3 million southern blacks were still not registered. The Selma campaign (see page 34) was designed to draw attention to this shameful fact (*Source 5*).

THE 1965 VOTING RIGHTS ACT

The violence in Selma led Johnson to prepare a watertight Voting Rights Bill, which became law in August 1965 (see page 35). The effects were immediate. In state after state, blacks were able to register without intimidation, and numbers on the voting rolls rose sharply (*Source 6*). In 1952, only 20 per cent of eligible southern blacks were registered. By the time of King's death in 1968, the figure was 60 per cent.

SUCCESS STORY

The 1964 Civil and 1965 Voting Rights Acts changed blacks' lives dramatically for the better. The former ended segregation, while increasing education and job opportunities. The latter allowed blacks to play their proper role in political life for the first time. Both were a clear success.

SOURCE 3

I shall ask the Congress... to make a commitment it has not fully made in this century to the proposition that race has no place in American life or law.
(EXTRACT FROM A TELEVISED ADDRESS MADE BY KENNEDY, 11 JUNE 1963)

SOURCE 4

SEC. 201 (a) All persons shall be entitled to the full and equal enjoyment of the goods, services, facilities, and privileges, advantages, and accommodations of any place of public accommodation, as defined in this section, without discrimination or segregation on the ground of race, color, religion, or national origin.
(EXTRACT FROM THE 1964 CIVIL RIGHTS ACT)

SOURCE 5

Why are we in jail? Have you ever been required to answer 100 questions on government, some abstruse [difficult to understand] even to a political scientist, merely to vote? Have you ever stood in line with over a hundred others and after waiting an entire day seen less than ten given the qualifying test? THIS IS SELMA, ALABAMA. THERE ARE MORE NEGROES IN JAIL WITH ME THAN THERE ARE ON THE VOTING ROLLS.
(EXTRACT FROM KING'S 'LETTER FROM SELMA JAIL', WHICH HE WROTE IN 1965 WHILE IMPRISONED IN SELMA, ALABAMA)

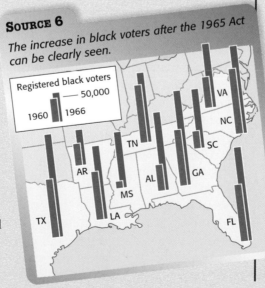

SOURCE 6

The increase in black voters after the 1965 Act can be clearly seen.

Registered black voters
— 50,000
1960 | 1966

VA
NC
SC
GA
TN
AL
AR
MS
LA
TX
FL

CIVIL RIGHTS LEGISLATION – SUCCESS OR FAILURE?

FAILURE?

SOURCE 7

[I deplore the] *timidity of the federal government that is willing to spend millions of dollars a day to defend freedom in Vietnam but cannot protect the rights of its citizens at home.*
(MARTIN LUTHER KING SPEAKING IN SELMA, ALABAMA, 1965)

SOURCE 8

...even if we pass this bill, the battle will not be over. What happened in Selma is part of a far larger movement...the effort of American Negroes to secure for themselves the full blessings of American life.
(PRESIDENT JOHNSON SPEAKING ON 15 MARCH 1965, THE DAY HE SUBMITTED THE VOTING RIGHTS BILL TO CONGRESS)

SOURCE 9

Laws are passed in a crisis mood after a Birmingham or a Selma, but no substantial fervor survives the formal signing of legislation. The recording of the law in itself is treated as the reality of the reform.
(MARTIN LUTHER KING)

SOURCE 10

US UNEMPLOYMENT
1963   4.8% white
        12.1% non-white

CHICAGO UNEMPLOYMENT
1966   2.3% overall
        13.0% black

THE BATTLE CONTINUES

The 1964 Civil Rights Act and 1965 Voting Rights Act were significant pieces of legislation. However, they were not always put into practice effectively, and failed to address many of the underlying problems faced by blacks in the USA. As a result, the black community had to continue its battles against discrimination long after the new laws were passed.

THEORY AND PRACTICE

The implementation of the 1964 Civil Rights Act was fraught with difficulty. Although it officially outlawed segregation, the unofficial separation of blacks and whites continued in many parts of the South, just as it did in the North. The law simply did not have the power to change the hearts and minds of whites who refused to believe blacks were their equals.

There was also a gap between the theory and practice of the 1965 Voting Rights Act. Both before and after its introduction, King criticized the federal government's failure to protect Southern blacks who tried to vote (*Source 7*). The rise in voter numbers from August 1965 was by no means wholly due to government enforcement of the new Act – thousands of blacks were persuaded to register for the first time by student volunteers who toured the South. The same volunteers also pressurized Congress to provide more registrars (see page 35).

Legislation did little to overcome poverty in black ghettos.

CONTINUING CONCERN

Both President Lyndon B. Johnson and Martin Luther King openly acknowledged the limitations of the new legislation (*Sources 8* and *9*). The riots in Los Angeles and other cities shortly after the Acts had passed into law (see page 36)

A policeman frisks rioters in Detroit, Michigan during a 1967 riot.

showed that their analysis was correct.

Over the following years, King repeatedly publicized the continuing problems of blacks, especially in the northern ghettos. They included poverty, run-down, overpriced accommodation and exclusion from better housing in white areas. Blacks also had to endure bad schools, inadequate health care and high unemployment (*Source 10*). King urged both governments and the public to assess the situation honestly, while Malcolm X cut to the heart of the matter with his usual candour (*Source 11*).

RIOT REPORT

From the mid-1960s, King campaigned for poor *urban* blacks, whom the Civil and Voting Rights Acts had scarcely affected. Black Power advocates used their own techniques in pursuit of the same goals. Progress was slow and unrest continued – there were 43 city riots in 1966, and eight more serious disturbances erupted in 1967. In response, Johnson ordered former Illinois governor Otto Kerner to chair an investigative commission. His 1968 report confirmed what King had long proclaimed (*Source 12*).

LIMITATIONS AND FAILURES

As King himself often pointed out, there are limits to what legislation can achieve. Although the Civil and Voting Rights Acts outlawed many forms of racial discrimination, they could not tackle deep-rooted social ills. In this sense, they failed black Americans and left many feeling that the federal government did not care about their plight (*Source 13*).

Otto Kerner led the commission on the origins of race riots.

SOURCE 11

In this year, 1965, I am certain that more – and worse – riots are going to erupt, in yet more cities, in spite of the conscience-salving Civil Rights Bill. The reason is that the cause of these riots, the racist malignancy in America, has been too long unattended.
(EXTRACT FROM *THE AUTOBIOGRAPHY OF MALCOLM X*)

SOURCE 12

What white Americans have never fully understood – but what the Negro can never forget – is that white society is deeply implicated in the ghetto. White institutions created it, white institutions maintain it, and white society condones it. Our society is moving toward two societies, one black, one white–separate but unequal.
(EXTRACT FROM THE 1968 REPORT OF THE NATIONAL ADVISORY COMMISSION ON CIVIL DISORDERS, CHAIRED BY OTTO KERNER)

SOURCE 13

I feel that the federal government have proven that it don't care about poor people. Everything that we have asked for through these years had been handed down on paper. It's never been a reality. We the poor people of Mississippi is tired. We're tired of it so we're going to build for ourselves, because we don't have a government that represents us.
(THE WORDS OF MRS UNITA BLACKWELL, A POOR BLACK WOMAN, IN 1966)

FIGHTING WAR AND POVERTY – RIGHT OR WRONG?

After the Civil and Voting Rights Acts passed into law, Martin Luther King still continued his campaigns on behalf of American blacks. At the same time, however, he began to address two other major issues – the USA's growing involvement in the Vietnam War and the plight of all the country's poor, from American Indians to Chicanos. In doing so, he earned far more criticism than acclaim, especially from the Johnson administration. So was King right to condemn war and fight poverty, or wrong to meddle in matters outside the area of black civil rights? Read both sides of the argument and the sources below, then judge for yourself.

RIGHT?

SOURCE 1

When he accepted the Nobel peace prize he baptized all races into his congregation and confirmed the world as the battle-ground for his gospel of nonviolence and reconciliation. He is no longer – and probably never can be – a spokesman for just an American Negro minority.
(EXTRACT FROM AN ARTICLE BY FORMER SCLC MEMBER CHARLES FAGER IN THE *CHRISTIAN CENTURY* MAGAZINE)

SOURCE 2

We have destroyed [Vietnamese peasants'] most cherished institutions – the family and the village. We have destroyed their land and their crops…We have corrupted their women and children and killed their men. What strange liberators we are!
(MARTIN LUTHER KING, SPEAKING ON 4 APRIL 1967)

ADDRESSING POVERTY

King began seriously to address the question of poverty in 1964. In his book *Why We Can't Wait*, he suggested creating a Bill of Rights for the Disadvantaged that would provide federal aid to all the USA's poor. In the same year, Johnson committed himself to the fight against poverty by introducing a range of education and welfare schemes. They were intended to create a 'Great Society' in which all Americans shared.

WORDS AGAINST WAR

For the next two years, King continued to devote himself mainly to the black cause, first in Selma, then in Chicago. But at the same time he began to speak out against Johnson's policy of increased intervention in the Vietnam War (see page 36). King saw this not so much as a radical new departure as an inevitable consequence of his belief in Christianity and non-violence. Many other people agreed (*Source 1*).

Robert Kennedy (see pages 27 and 28) also spoke out against poverty and against the Vietnam War.

WHERE DO WE GO FROM HERE?

In 1967, King began to address his two new themes – poverty across the race divide and Vietnam – in earnest. The poverty issue was much in his mind early in the year when he went to Jamaica to write a book. Called *Where Do We Go From Here?* (see page 38), it encouraged the poor of all colours and creeds to unite in the struggle for justice. Back in the USA, King's preaching began to incorporate such ideas, too.

ANTI-WAR ACTIVITIES

Before King launched an all-out campaign against poverty however, he turned his attention to Vietnam. Watching the horrors of the war on television convinced him he should be making greater efforts to end the fighting. So from early 1967 he repeatedly denounced the conflict, most devastatingly in an address at Riverside Church, New York on 4 April (see page 38 and *Source 2*). These activities brought condemnation – from politicians, conservative blacks in the SCLC and NAACP and the press. But King had no doubt his actions were morally right (*Source 3*).

Facing opposition to his Vietnam policy, President Johnson did not stand for re-election in 1968.

THE POOR PEOPLE'S CAMPAIGN

By the summer of 1967 it was clear that, despite the 'Great Society' programme, the American poor were still in dire need. In addition, government money that might have helped them was being spent on Vietnam. King therefore decided to launch the Poor People's Campaign of which he had long dreamed (see page 39 and *Source 4*). His plan was that 3,000 people should march to Washington D.C. in 1968. Once there they would hold mass demonstrations and demand introduction of the Bill of Rights he had proposed. Tragically King did not live to see his dream fulfilled.

THE RIGHT WAY

King's activities after the Civil and Voting Rights Acts became law were a continuation of his earlier work. He saw it as his Christian duty to fight for justice wherever and whenever the need arose, so it was right and logical for him to struggle against both war and poverty. As he stated in his 'Drum Major Instinct' sermon, his aim was simply to serve (*Source 5*).

SOURCE 3

Now there are those who say, 'You are a civil rights leader. What are you doing speaking out [against the Vietnam War]? You should stay in your field.' Well, I wish you would go back and tell them for me that before I became a civil rights leader, I was a preacher of the Gospel...
(MARTIN LUTHER KING SPEAKING AT VICTORY BAPTIST CHURCH, LOS ANGELES)

SOURCE 4

Gentlemen....we're going to reach out to the poor people in all directions in this country...And we're going to bring them together and enlarge this campaign into something bigger than just a civil-rights movement for Negroes.
(MARTIN LUTHER KING SPEAKING TO SCLC STAFF IN NOVEMBER 1967)

SOURCE 5

Every now and then I think about my own death, and I think about my own funeral...I want you to say that day I tried to be right on the war question...I want you to say that I tried to love and serve humanity. Yes, if you want to say that I was a drum major, say that I was a drum major for justice. Say that I was a drum major for peace. That I was a drum major for righteousness.
(MARTIN LUTHER KING SPEAKING AT EBENEZER CHURCH, 4 FEBRUARY 1968)

FIGHTING WAR AND POVERTY – RIGHT OR WRONG?

WRONG?

SOURCE 6

If we are not with him [Johnson] on Vietnam, then he is not going to be with us on civil rights.
(WHITNEY YOUNG OF THE NATIONAL URBAN LEAGUE, SPEAKING TO KING)

SOURCE 7

Is he casting about for a role in Vietnam because the civil rights struggle is no longer adequate to his own estimate of his talents?
(EXTRACT FROM AN ARTICLE BY AMERICAN JOURNALIST MAX FREEDMAN)

SOURCE 8

At the end of October [1965]…the Bureau [FBI] requested another six-month authorization for wiretaps on SCLC's Atlanta headquarters. The intercepts, the Bureau told the Attorney General, had "provided considerable valuable intelligence information concerning communist influence on the SCLC through King, as well as the communist influence evident in the outspoken position which King has taken in opposition to the United States foreign policy concerning Vietnam."
(EXTRACT FROM *THE FBI AND MARTIN LUTHER KING, JR.* BY DAVID J. GARROW)

MISGUIDED ACTIVITIES

By deciding to tackle war and poverty from the mid-1960s, King alienated large sections of American society. At the same time, his misguided new activities cast doubt on his own integrity, on his commitment to non-violence and on the validity of his previous civil rights achievements.

THE VIETNAM QUESTION

Nowhere was King more misguided than on the Vietnam question. Before he first spoke out, in 1965, SCLC advisers warned him it would be foolish to do so. In their view, criticism of American foreign policy would anger the President and reduce his support for the civil rights cause (*Source 6*). The public, then largely in favour of the war, might also react badly, and so their contributions to SCLC funds decrease.

Despite the warnings, King went ahead with his denunciations of the war. The results were even worse than predicted: Johnson and many Congress members were furious, while journalists wrote that sheer vanity had deluded King into believing he could influence world politics (*Source 7*). J. Edgar Hoover (see page 28) and the FBI stepped up surveillance of King, falsely claiming he was influenced by Communists (*Source 8*).

BITTER BACKLASH

When King increased his attacks in 1967, the backlash was even more bitter. After the Riverside Church speech, Johnson received a damning report on King from an advisor. Many newspapers were equally critical, claiming King did not know what he was talking about (*Source 9*). Even black leaders such as Roy Wilkins of the NAACP refused to back

NAACP director Roy Wilkins disagreed with King's anti-Vietnam War stance.

him. King's outspokenness made little difference to the war, but did affect the civil rights movement. Once a supporter, Johnson became distant, for example ignoring King's advice on the 1967 riots (see page 39).

THE POOR PEOPLE'S CAMPAIGN

King's commitment to the Poor People's Campaign proved equally disastrous. When he first decided to go ahead, in 1967, SCLC members warned him of the potential pitfalls – the huge cost, the difficulty of organizing such a vast operation (*Source 10*) and the possibility that it would unleash terrible violence that he could not control. President Johnson, meanwhile, expressed his outrage at the prospect, and the FBI, fearing a 'true black revolution', began to watch King even more closely. He chose to ignore all these warning signs.

The Poor People's Campaign went ahead after King's death. A tent city was set up in Washington, but little was achieved.

King's participation in the Memphis rubbish collectors' strike of 1968 (see page 40) was intended in part to be a miniature trial run for the Washington campaign. Sadly, it brought his movement into yet more disrepute (*Source 11*). His return to Memphis in April was designed to show that non-violent protest could work. But it was already too late.

THE WRONG WAY

In concerning himself with war and poverty from 1965, King made a major error of judgement. Not only did he stray dangerously beyond his area of expertise, he also seriously damaged the civil rights movement and tarnished his own reputation. He had chosen the wrong way forward.

SOURCE 9

The Washington Post stated that King's criticism included "sheer inventions of unsupported fantasy"... By uttering "bitter and damaging allegations and inferences that he did not and could not document," the Post added, King "has done a grave injury to those who are his natural allies... and...an even greater injury to himself. Many who have listened to him with respect will never again accord him the same confidence. He has diminished his usefulness to his cause, to his country and to his people."
(EXTRACT FROM *THE FBI AND MARTIN LUTHER KING, JR.* BY DAVID J. GARROW)

SOURCE 10

You are attempting the impossible. There is no way for Martin Luther King to bring white poor, Puerto Rican poor, black poor, Irish poor together in any meaningful way.
(KING ADVISOR BAYARD RUSTIN)

SOURCE 11

Dr King's pose as a leader of a non-violent movement has been shattered. He now has the entire nation doubting his word when he insists that his April [Washington] project can be peaceful.
(EXTRACT FROM A MEMPHIS NEWSPAPER QUOTED IN *MARTIN LUTHER KING JR., AND THE CIVIL RIGHTS MOVEMENT IN AMERICA* BY JOHN WHITE)

FREE AT LAST – REALITY OR ILLUSION?

'Free at Last, Free At Last, Thank God Almighty, I'm Free At Last.'
These words from a spiritual are carved on Martin Luther King's tomb
in South View Cemetery, Atlanta. But did the civil rights movement that he
led so skilfully and at such personal cost really bring freedom to black
Americans? And if so, have they been able to maintain and develop it in
the three decades and more since King's death? Read both sides of the
argument and the sources below, then judge for yourself.

REALITY?

SOURCE 1

...the obligation of every
school district is to terminate
dual school systems at once.
(EXTRACT FROM A RULING OF THE
US SUPREME COURT, 1969)

SOURCE 2

US BLACK PUPILS IN
SEGREGATED SCHOOLS (%)

| 1968 | 64 |
| 1991 | 34 |

SOURCE 3

BLACK PEOPLE IN
WHITE-COLLAR JOBS (%)

| 1960 | 17 |
| 1976 | 33 |

SOURCE 4

Among the EEOC's recent
litigation achievements are:
...over 5,000 entry level
and 34 management
trainee job offers to
qualified African American,
Hispanic, and female
applicants previously
denied positions.
(EXTRACT FROM THE EQUAL
EMPLOYMENT OPPORTUNITY
COMMISSION WEBSITE)

A GREAT ACHIEVEMENT

It was Martin Luther King's abiding achievement to establish
a legal framework that made freedom a possibility for all black
Americans. They have since continued the struggle to
make it an everyday reality.

DESEGREGATING SCHOOLS

A major advance
occurred just a year after
King's death. By then,
Richard Nixon was
President, and the 1964
Civil Rights Act was taking
effect. Some school
districts continued to block
desegregation, however, so
the US Supreme Court ruled
that there should be no more delays (*Source 1*). As many
schools were in all-white or all-black areas busing – that is, the
transportation of pupils by bus from one district to another –
was introduced to help ensure a racial mix (*Source 2*).

King's tomb in Atlanta, inscribed
with the words 'Free At Last'.

AFFIRMATIVE ACTION

In the 1960s, universities, businesses and many other American
institutions began to run affirmative action programmes.
Their aim was to help blacks and other minorities into higher
education and work, both by encouraging them to apply and
by making entry requirements less strict. Some institutions also
introduced quota systems. Affirmative action achieved results.
The number of black people going to college, as well as the
percentage in office jobs, quickly soared (*Source 3*).

JUDGE
FOR YOURSELF

George W. Bush with Colin Powell.

HIGH-PROFILE POSITIONS

Black Americans have also become far more visible in the national life of the USA, not only in the fields of music and sport, to which they have often felt confined by white expectations, but also in business, the arts and politics. Colin Powell and Condoleezza Rice were both appointed Secretary of State under George W. Bush's government. Barack Obama was the Democratic candidate for the 2008 presidential election.

THE EQUAL EMPLOYMENT OPPORTUNITY COMMISSION (EEOC)

The EEOC established by the 1964 Civil Rights Act (see page 34) still fights against discrimination on behalf of black people and other minorities (*Source 4*). In February 1996, it introduced a new National Enforcement Plan to increase its effectiveness. On 21 November 1991, Congress also passed a new Civil Rights Act that strengthened the legal provisions against racial discrimination in the workplace (*Source 5*).

SIGNS AND SYMBOLS

Both federal and state governments have made important gestures acknowledging black contributions to American life and drawing a line under past discrimination. In 1983, for example, Congress made 15 January, King's birthday, a national holiday. More recently, some southern states have reduced the size of the Confederate Flag (see page 11) on their state flags as a sign that racism has no place in today's USA (*Source 6*).

A poster in favour of Georgia's old flag, which was later changed.

FREE AT LAST

Since the 1960s, black Americans have made great strides towards achieving the freedom that they have sought since the slavery era. They have not yet reached all their goals, but are free to do so, as the great progress they have made demonstrates.

SOURCE 5

An Act
To amend the Civil Rights Act of 1964 to strengthen and improve Federal civil rights laws, to provide for damages in cases of intentional employment discrimination…and for other purposes…
(EXTRACT FROM THE CIVIL RIGHTS ACT OF 1991)

SOURCE 6

…I am…proud that we have come so far that my children find it hard to believe that we ever had segregated schools or separate water fountains labeled 'white' and 'colored'. And I am proud that these changes came about because unity prevailed over division. Today, that same unity must be exercised again. The Confederate Battle Flag occupies two-thirds of our current state flag. Some argue that it is a symbol of segregation, defiance, and white supremacy, others that it is a testament to a brave and valiant people who were willing to die to defend their homes and health. I am not here to settle this argument…but I am here because it is time to end it… Adopt [the new] flag and our people will be united as one rather than divided by race and hatred.
(GEORGIA GOVERNOR ROY BARNES SPEAKING ON 25 JANUARY 2001. THE STATE ADOPTED A NEW FLAG SIX DAYS LATER)

FREE AT LAST – REALITY OR ILLUSION?

ILLUSION?

SOURCE 7

When Resurrection City closed down there was a sense of betrayal, a sense of abandonment. The dreamer [King] had been killed in Memphis and there was an attempt now to kill the dream itself...
(REVEREND JESSE JACKSON, SPEAKING ABOUT THE 'TENT CITY' IN WASHINGTON – SEE PAGE 57)

SOURCE 8

...there goes all the progress, everything that's happened in the past ten years.
(OPINION OF A BLACK WORKER ON THE BAKKE RULING)

SOURCE 9

[t]he state shall not discriminate against or grant preferential treatment to, any individual or group on the basis of race, sex, color, ethnicity, or national origin in the operation of public employment, public education, or public contracting.
(EXTRACT FROM PROPOSITION 209)

SOURCE 10

UNEMPLOYMENT (%)

	Black	White
1980	14.5	6.1
1990	11.8	4.8
1994	13.9	6.7

(US ECONOMICS AND STATISTICS ADMINISTRATION DATA)

FADING DREAMS

Black Americans' dreams of freedom began to fade straight after King's 1968 assassination. Ralph Abernathy (see page 20), King's successor, had neither his talents nor his charisma, and was unable to bring the Poor People's Campaign to a successful conclusion (*Source 7*). The riots that took place after King's death also signalled a return to the past.

BUSING

The situation did not improve. Busing programmes designed to integrate schools were often opposed by whites. Parents in Boston and Denver, for example, protested violently against local schemes, and as a result Nixon tried to introduce an anti-busing bill. In the *Milliken* v. *Bradley* case of 1974, the US Supreme Court ruled a Detroit busing scheme unconstitutional because it stopped parents having control over schools. Rich whites often simply avoided the issue by choosing private education for their children.

AFFIRMATIVE ACTION

Affirmative action programmes have been similarly blocked. In a celebrated legal case, white American Allan Bakke took the University of California to court. He had failed to gain a place at its School of Medicine in 1973, but later learned that black students with lower test scores had been admitted and that the 'special admissions program' had only ever accepted blacks. As a result, Bakke claimed to be a victim of racial discrimination.

In 1995, the Nation of Islam (see page 48) organized a 'Million-Man March' to Washington D.C. to protest against continuing racism.

In 1978, the US Supreme Court ruled in his favour. Many advocates of affirmative action were horrified (*Source 8*).

In 1997, the Supreme Court reached a decision on another major case. It allowed the addition to the California constitution of Proposition 209, which banned affirmative action in the public domain (*Source 9*).

LIFE AND LAW

The fact that a few black Americans have made their mark in public life cannot disguise the truth that most live far less well than their white counterparts. For example, black unemployment is higher (*Source 10*), black earning power lower (*Source 11*) and black life expectancy shorter than white (*Source 12*). In the ghettos, where drug addiction and violence are rife, many young blacks now look to Malcolm X not King for inspiration (*Source 13*), and express their rage through rap lyrics.

Discrimination against blacks by the police and legal system also remains a major problem (*Source 14*). The most serious case of recent years was that of Rodney King, a black man beaten by Los Angeles police in 1991. A member of the public videoed the incident, which was shown on television. When a jury found the police not guilty of brutality the following year, riots broke out, leading to the deaths of 53 people.

Rioting in Los Angeles following the 1992 verdict in the Rodney King case (see text).

FAR FROM FREEDOM

King said: 'Justice for black people will not flow into society merely from court decisions…White America must recognize that justice for black people cannot be achieved without radical changes in the structure of our society.' As many of those changes have yet to be made, justice, and the freedom that it makes possible, have yet to be achieved.

SOURCE 11

AVERAGE ANNUAL SALARY 1991

Black college graduates $30,910

White college graduates $37,490

(US CENSUS BUREAU DATA)

SOURCE 12

MALE LIFE EXPECTANCY

	White	Black
1980	63	59
1985	74.6	65

(FIGURES TAKEN FROM *MAKING MALCOLM* BY MICHAEL ERIC DYSON)

SOURCE 13

Everybody still listens to Malcolm X. When he talks you can't walk away. The thing about X is that he attracted and still attracts the people who have given up and lives recklessly – the crowd that just don't care what's going on. Making a difference in these people's lives is truly the essence of Malcolm X.

(RAPPERS ULTRAMAGNETIC MC'S)

SOURCE 14

In Boston in April 1970, a policeman shot and killed an unarmed black man, a patient in a ward in the Boston City Hospital, firing five shots after the black man snapped a towel at him. The chief judge of the municipal court of Boston exonerated the policeman.

(CASE QUOTED IN *A PEOPLE'S HISTORY OF THE UNITED STATES* BY HOWARD ZINN)

GLOSSARY

affirmative action Action designed to counteract discrimination against disadvantaged groups. Affirmative action programmes often include schemes to help black people acquire jobs or college places by making entry requirements less rigid than for whites.

Attorney General The chief law officer of the American federal government and head of the Justice Department.

Black Muslims A black religious movement established in the USA in 1930, and led from 1934 by Elijah Muhammad. Although Elijah Muhammad taught that black Americans were descended from a Muslim tribe, his teachings differed in many ways from orthodox Islam. More recently, the group has divided into two factions, one holding firm to Elijah Muhammad's teachings and the other embracing Islam proper. The movement's alternative name is the Nation of Islam.

boycott A protest that involves refusing to participate in an activity or to buy a product. The aim of a boycott is usually to cause disruption or loss of earnings and so persuade authorities to introduce change.

busing The practice of transporting children by bus between US schools in an effort to ensure racial integration among pupils.

Chicano A Mexican-American.

civil rights The personal rights of citizens that guarantee them certain freedoms, usually including freedom of speech and religion. In the USA, many civil rights are listed in the Bill of Rights, 10 amendments to the Constitution that were adopted in 1791. King fought in particular to ensure that the additional rights outlined in the 13th, 14th and 15th Amendments (see pages 11 and 16) were extended to black people.

colony A territory governed by the rulers of another state.

Communist A person who supports the political and economic system known as Communism. Communism aims to create a classless society in which power and money are shared. Communist countries, such as the former Soviet Union and present-day China, are ruled by unelected members of just one political party. Communist businesses are run by the state rather than by private individuals.

Confederacy The seven, later 11 states of the American South that broke away from the USA in 1861, so provoking civil war. The war ended in 1865, when northern Union forces defeated the Confederacy.

Congress The law-making body of the USA. It consists of two houses, the Senate and the House of Representatives.

Deep South The south-eastern US states of South Carolina, Georgia, Alabama, Mississippi and Louisiana, which are considered most typical of the South as a whole.

Democratic Party One of the two major political parties in the USA. The Democratic Party was founded in 1792, and provided many early presidents. However, it was deeply divided over slavery and after the Civil War lost much of its influence to the Republican Party. During the 1930s and '40s, under the leadership of President Franklin D. Roosevelt, the Democratic Party became more liberal. Presidents Kennedy and Johnson, both supporters of Martin Luther King, were Democrats.

disenfranchisement Inability to vote, generally caused by either legal restrictions or intimidation.

divinity *See* **theology**.

draft card An official US document that requires a person to report for compulsory military service.

Executive Order An order made by a US President that does not have to be approved by Congress.

FBI (Federal Bureau of Investigation) An organization whose main role is to prevent spies and other enemies of the government from operating within the USA, but that may also investigate violations of particular federal laws. The FBI is part of the Department of Justice.

federal marshal A law enforcement agent whose main role is to protect the federal courts and to make sure that the US judicial system works effectively. Some marshals also have wider law enforcement powers, including a duty to keep the peace.

filibuster A deliberate attempt to prevent the passage of a bill through Congress by using delaying tactics such as lengthy speeches.

First World War A major war that lasted from 1914 to 1918 and involved many countries. The USA joined the war in 1917, fighting alongside Britain and France and (briefly) Russia to defeat Germany and Austria-Hungary. By 1918, more than 450,000 black people had moved from the American South to the North to take up wartime jobs in factories and mines.

grandfather clause A law in some southern US states that was designed to allow illiterate white people to vote while preventing black people from doing so. Such clauses exempted people who had the right to vote on 1 January 1867, as well as their descendants, from electoral literacy tests. Since former slaves had not been granted the vote by that date, they had to take the tests and so were still effectively disenfranchised.

Great Depression, the The period of high unemployment and economic weakness that began with the 1929 collapse of the US stock market in Wall Street, New York. Much of Europe was also affected. The Depression had eased by 1934, but did not fully end until the Second World War era.

inaugurate To install (e.g. a president) in office with a formal ceremony. US Presidents are normally elected in November, then inaugurated in January the following year.

Kingdom of God According to Christian teaching, the reign of God on Earth, made possible through people's obedience to His will.

Nation of Islam *See* **Black Muslims**

National Guard The military force of each individual US state. National Guards may be called on to undertake federal service (service for the USA as a whole), in which case they become part of the US Army.

Nazi A member of the National Socialist German Workers' Party, which ruled Germany during the Second World War under the leadership of Adolf Hitler. 'Nazi' is a short form of the German words for 'National Socialist'.

pacifist Of or relating to the belief that violence of any kind, including war, is wrong.

penitentiary The normal US word for a prison where serious criminals are confined.

Ph.D. The highest academic degree, which is awarded for original research. The abbreviation stands for Latin words meaning 'Doctor of Philosophy'.

poll tax A tax collected from every adult, irrespective of wealth, property owned or income.

quota system A system of allocating jobs, college places or similar in which a fixed proportion (quota) of jobs or places is allocated to a particular group, e.g. black people.

Reconstruction The period of US history that immediately followed the American Civil War and lasted from 1865 to 1877. During Reconstruction, the southern states rejoined the Union and rebuilt their war-torn territories. At first, the status of black people in the South also improved, thanks largely to pressure from the federal government. But by the end of the era, when federal troops withdrew from the South, racial discrimination was steadily worsening once more.

Reformation, the The religious movement that began in 16th-century Germany as an attempt to reform some practices of the Roman Catholic Church. Eventually it became more wide-ranging and led to the establishment of Protestant churches. Martin Luther (1483–1546) was a major leader of the Reformation.

Republican Party One of the two major political parties in the USA. The Republican Party was formed in 1854 and the first Republican president, Abraham Lincoln, elected in 1860. Lincoln's anti-slavery stance precipitated the American Civil War. After the war, Republicans remained dominant in the USA until Franklin D. Roosevelt was elected in 1932 (*see* **Democratic Party**). Twenty years later, after the Second World War, military hero and Democrat Dwight D. Eisenhower became President. But he did little to further the civil rights cause.

Second World War A major war that lasted from 1939 to 1945 and involved many countries. The USA entered the war in 1941, after the Japanese bombed a US naval base in Pearl Harbor, Hawaii. It then joined Britain, France and Russia to defeat Germany, Japan and their allies.

secular Non-religious.

seminary An institution where people train to become priests, ministers or rabbis.

separatism A doctrine which teaches that people belonging to different racial, religious or other groups should live in separate communities.

sharecropper A farmer who works land rented from its owner in return for a share of the crop produced. Many former slaves became sharecroppers on white-owned land after slavery was abolished, so often remained largely under white control.

state capitol A building in which the law-making body of a US state government meets.

tenement A small room or flat in a large building containing many similar homes. Tenements are usually rented rather than bought.

theology The study of God and religious doctrine, especially with regard to a particular religion such as Christianity. Another name for theology is **divinity**.

US Supreme Court The highest federal (national) court in the USA. It is made up of nine judges and its rulings are final.

Vietnam War The war between Communist North Vietnam and non-Communist South Vietnam that began in the 1950s. The USA backed South Vietnam from the outset, but did not send in large numbers of troops until the mid-1960s. Following heavy losses, sections of the US public called for an end to the war. In 1973, a ceasefire was signed and US troops withdrew. In 1975, North Vietnam defeated South Vietnam.

INDEX